WHEN
GHOSTS
SPEAK

WHEN
GHOSTS
SPEAK

UNDERSTANDING THE WORLD OF
EARTHBOUND SPIRITS

MARY ANN WINKOWSKI

HODDER
MOBIUS

First published in Great Britain in 2008 by Mobius
An imprint of Hodder & Stoughton
An Hachette Livre UK company

1

A CIP catalogue record for this title is available from the British Library

ISBN 978 0 340 96102 5
Printed and bound by Mackays of Chatham Ltd, Chatham, Kent

Hodder & Stoughton policy is to use papers that are natural, renewable and recyclable products
and made from wood grown in sustainable forests. The logging and manufacturing processes are
expected to conform to the environmental regulations of the country of origin.

Hodder & Stoughton Ltd
338 Euston Road
London NW1 3BH

www.hodder.co.uk

This book is for my loving husband, Ted,
my best friend for over forty years.

Our daughters, Amber and Tara,
who were great children and are now exceptional adults.

In memory of my grandmother Marie Fantozzi.
She recognized my abilities, nurtured them,
and gave me invaluable advice up until her death in 1998.

To all the earthbound spirits I have met over the last fifty years
who have educated me and taught me how to accept and
enjoy my unique life, as I helped them on their journeys.

Although I have encountered each living individual and each earth-bound spirit who appears in this book, I strongly feel that it is important to protect the privacy of both the living and the dead. Therefore, names, locations, and certain identifying characteristics have been changed throughout.

Contents

PART III
LIVING WITH GHOSTS

Foreword

I HAVE BEEN seeing spirits and professionally communicating with them for more than twenty-five years, and the only time I have ever heard of a ghostbuster was watching Dan Aykroyd battle with slime in the *Ghostbuster* movies. For many years, I have met people claiming they had the ability to clear houses and detach unwanted entities, and being somewhat skeptical of individuals making such claims, I must follow an absolute unscientific method of testing them. Why *unscientific*? you might ask. I guess because as of now, scientists cannot correctly measure spirits or ghosts based on the limited instrumentation they have currently developed. To date, the most they can demonstrate are temperature changes, energy spikes, and luminous orbs. So when people tell me they can communicate with ghosts or spirits, I tell them they will have to prove it to me by giving specific names, details, and information that they could not find on the Internet or in other ways. When I had the opportunity to meet Mary Ann, I was all prepared with an ounce of skepticism and my sharpened intuitive skills. Was she genuine? Did she give facts she could not have gleaned elsewhere? Did she have integrity and a sense of responsibility for her work? Would she be aided by any gadgets or machines such as night-vision goggles or even a Dan Aykroyd slime-away machine?

Mary Ann was nothing like I expected. She didn't go into a trance or dance around and chant some ancient cultural ritualistic prayer or even carry instruments, aside from a notebook and pen. She was, well . . . normal. In fact, very normal. Instead of Dan Aykroyd, I saw an engaging Midwestern homemaker who would seem more comfortable making brownies than chasing after otherworldly phantoms. But don't get me wrong: Just because she has a sweet disposition doesn't mean she is anybody's fool. She carries weapons—with her wits, her ability, and one forceful look in the right direction, she can scare a ghost right out of its earthly lodging and scrambling toward the Light.

Through movies and television, ghosts have been portrayed as everything from white-sheeted figures to foggy clouds and monstrous cadavers, leering at, frightening, and downright scaring humans, who seem panicked and hopeless against their onslaught. Through the media, we have gleaned that earthbound spirits are supposed to be physically monstrous, obnoxious, and suffering from a horrible memory loss. They have also been portrayed as evil and demonic. Well, while these traits may work really well when creating ways to frighten an audience, it seems that in most cases the picture is very far from the truth. Yes, occasionally there might be a ghost who seems to be quite unevolved and relentless, but you must remember: Ghosts are merely human beings who have died. They don't take on monster masks when they die and don't seem to replace their clothes with white sheets.

From my experiences of being present with Mary Ann when she works, it seems that ghosts are very good at remembering their birth and death dates, know where they are buried, can easily recall their earthly employments and interests, and most of the time, have some type of unfinished earthly business. They stay here because they want more sensations of the physical world, are perhaps afraid of what awaits them in the afterlife, or most often are just plain nosy. They are no longer restrained by their bodies or the laws of the physical dimension, so they can snoop around—and would rather do so than spend a day in paradise.

The interesting part of this subject matter, which fascinates me, is that these types of ghosts are quite a bit different from the ones I communicate with. A distinction should be made. The ones I work with have already passed into the Light and come back to give messages of love and forgiveness, with the occasional regrets thrown in. But they are never stuck here and have never once said to me, *Boy, do I miss that physical world—I wish I could go back*. They are happy to be gone and only want their loved ones to know that they have survived and are very much a part of their lives, now helping them from a spiritual perspective. The ones who choose to stay here or who get caught here by their own greed, possessiveness, or fear are very different. It seems that they are lost between time and place. They are not here to help people but are more involved in fulfilling their earthly interests and delights. They pull energy from us and many times will try to upset our environment, so we will get upset and in turn feed their energy with our anger, helping them to stay here. When spirits are in the Light, they can come in a light body (which is a replica of the physical body), visiting us and influencing our lives in positive ways. I have also seen light beings attempt to help ghosts or earthbounds, and sometimes if the ghosts are ready and open they will hear them and may think about moving on. But getting through to a ghost is difficult from the spiritual dimensions because the ghost's mind-set is so tied to the earthly level.

Mary Ann's work in the realm of spirits is very important, because it provides a service not only to the living, but also to wayward ghosts, who many times feel a sense of abandonment and might think this is all there is to life outside the physical shell. She provides them a sense of freedom from the darkness—a new life they might not have been ready to see or experience. Interestingly enough, we can also draw an analogy to other living people walking on this earth who are caught up with physical things: power, possessiveness, greed, hatred, religion, and so on . . . Once they step out of living a life chained to those belief systems and direct their minds and hearts toward love, generosity, and joy, they begin to open up to the true nature of their spirits. They begin to see themselves as great spiritual beings first and foremost, and enjoy a freedom of mind they have never had before. They begin to finally understand that they are made from the spark of the God light, and that light is love.

So with the realization and awareness that you are a spiritual being and that this earth is only a temporary school in which to learn lessons and demonstrate love, when it is your turn to pass out of the body, you will hopefully be aware that there is a much better place to go to and will not need to stay around rattling pots and pans and spying on your neighbor. And in the meantime, if your home seems a little off and you have unending plumbing problems, car problems, or electrical upsets, the kids seem to have unexplained earaches, and the dog is acting restless, you just might have an unwanted visitor walking through and spying on you. Take a good look at yourself in the mirror and ask, *Who are you going to call?*

James Van Praagh, spiritual medium and
author of *Talking to Heaven*

PART I

Listening to Spirits

INTRODUCTION

The Ghost Phenomenon

So . . . IS ANYONE here now?" Jennifer Love Hewitt sat across from me, pouring a cup of tea. We were in her kitchen, and Love (as she prefers to be called) was meeting with me as she prepared to begin the first season of shooting what would become the CBS hit series *Ghost Whisperer*. I wanted to pinch myself. Me, a fifty-something housewife from Cleveland, was sitting and casually chatting with a well-known actress, sipping tea in her sun-filled kitchen on a summer afternoon. I was there because Love's character on the show, Melinda Gordon, can see and communicate with earthbound spirits. And so can I.

"There are two spirits here," I told her.

"What do you do next?" Love asked me. Although we'd known we'd be working together on *Ghost Whisperer*, this was the first time we had met, and I felt her studying me closely.

"Well, you can ask them questions," I told her. "When you're ready for them to leave, I can make the white Light and let them cross over. And then they'll be gone."

Like most people I work with, Love had all kinds of questions, both for me and for the spirits sharing her home. And although she couldn't see or hear her ghostly housemates, I could see them as plainly as I saw her, and they were more than happy to talk with me.

"Tell me who's here," she said.

"Well, there's a woman over there," I said, gesturing at the doorway. "She says she's Lon Chaney Jr.'s ex-wife."

Love looked startled. "Lon Chaney Jr. used to own this house! How did you know that?"

I wasn't surprised she wanted to know. I'd been asked this kind of question literally hundred of times; it's as if people suspect I have some previous knowledge of their lives and circumstances. Each time I patiently explain that I'm not a psychic. I can't read minds or see into the future. I can only tell them what a spirit tells me. And that's what I told Love.

"Well then, ask her how she likes my singing," Love said with a grin.

It seemed like a strange question, but when I looked over at the ghost, she was smiling. "She's having a bit of fun with you," the ghost told me. "She's a wonderful singer. She has recordings and everything."

Love asked a few more questions, we all chatted pleasantly, the spirit admitted she was ready to go into the Light, and I helped her leave.

Then Love asked, "Who else is here?"

I hesitated. All my years of experience told me that this next encounter wasn't going to be as pleasant as our chat with the former Mrs. Chaney. But in my work I've learned not to venture my opinion unless directly asked. "There's a youngish man here, too," I said.

The ghost, probably about thirty, with neatly cut light brown hair and an athletic build, lounged insolently in a corner. He stared at me in a way that was far from welcoming.

Again, Love had a lot of questions. But this time, her queries became very specific, very quickly. When people ask me to talk with the ghosts in their homes, it can seem a lot like a game of Twenty Questions: What's your name? How old are you? Where did you live? How did you die? People are naturally curious, and there's something about asking questions of someone they can't see or hear, but who has been sharing their home and watching their routines, sometimes for years, that makes them bolder than they might be if they'd simply met at a cocktail party.

Because this ghost was close to Love's age, she was curious to see if they had anything in common. As the story unraveled, it became more and more interesting. The man admitted that he had gone to the same high school she did. A few years ahead of her, but still . . . He told her that he admired her work. He could name all the movies she'd done, and all the television shows she'd been on. He'd been killed in a collision, he said. The more we talked, the more uncomfortable I became. While he was being straightforward with his answers, they were all delivered with a smirk. If I'd met him when he was alive, I'd have called him a creep. Dead, he was no different.

Love obviously felt uncomfortable, too. She excused herself for a few minutes, and when she came back into the room her expression was thoughtful.

"Does he watch me when I'm in the shower?" she blurted out.

Hoo-boy, I thought. I knew the answer to this one without even having to ask. With the smirk spreading wider across his face, the ghost replied that he sure did. I didn't bother relaying his enthusiasm, just nodded.

"He's a pervert!" Love was disgusted, though she couldn't help laughing at the situation. I'd already told her that most earth-bound spirits couldn't touch or harm people.

"He sure is," I agreed.

It was clearly time to let this Peeping Tom go into the Light.

"You really don't want her to think of you as a pervert, do you?" I said.

The ghost winced. It seemed as if I had managed to appeal to whatever moral standards this guy had.

"And now that she knows what you're up to, it's really not going to be that much fun for you anymore, is it?" I continued.

His shoulders slumped, and I knew he wasn't going to argue with me. I made the white Light and watched him walk into it.

"He's gone now," I told Love.

While the circumstances under which I was talking to these ghosts were special, there was nothing remarkable to me about the encounter. As I've said, I simply take what spirits tell me as fact. Over the fifty years that I've been doing this work, I've talked to so many spirits—nearly all of them strangers to me—that I tend not to think about them once they have gone into the Light.

What I sometimes forget is that while I may take my unusual ability for granted, very few others do.

The next morning, I was sitting in a conference room on the Paramount lot. It would be the first time that the writers and stars of the show were meeting. I knew that many of the writers were skeptical about what I could do. In fact, later that day all twelve of them, the producers, Love, and I were going to pile into a tour bus and take a "Ghost Tour" of some houses so they could *all* watch me at work.

I wasn't nervous about the upcoming tour. I'm used to dealing with skeptical people. In fact, it doesn't bother me at all. I've no need to convince anyone that I can communicate with earthbound spirits. If I worried about what other people thought of what I do, the past fifty years or so would have been stressful indeed. But when it came down to talking about my work with twelve Hollywood writers who had probably heard all kinds of stories in their careers, I kind of felt like it might matter a little that they believed in me. Still, I vowed to stick by my philosophy: *This is what I do. Believe in it or not, as you wish.* All of this was running through my mind when Love came into the conference room.

"Heard you got your place ghostbusted yesterday," one of the lead writers drawled, clearly hoping she'd have a snappy comeback.

Instead Love told everyone what had happened the previous day—how there had been two spirits and how one had been a creepy pervert. Now, I have found that most people exaggerate when they recount their ghost stories, but Love just stuck to the facts. Then she stepped over behind me and put her hands on my shoulders.

"Mary Ann doesn't even know this," she announced. And she proceeded to tell the writers what had happened *after* I left her house.

As you might imagine, she just hadn't been able to get the creepy guy out of her mind. So she called some old girlfriends from high school.

"That name just rang a bell with me," she explained.

Later that night, she got another call from a friend who had managed to talk to someone who had known her ghost when he was alive. What he'd neglected to mention in the conversations I'd had with him was that he'd been living in the basement of his parents' house when he died. When they went into his room to clean it out, his family and friends discovered a whole wall papered with photos of Love.

It makes sense, I thought as everyone else in the room stared at Love. The guy was literally a stalker while he was alive. How much easier had it been for him once he was dead?

"At least he won't be rattling around in my kitchen anymore," Love joked, breaking the tension in the room.

Later that day, we piled in and out of the tour bus and I talked to the various spirits in the different houses the producers selected. And while I still got tons of questions from the writers— who, by the way, ask more questions than detectives, and I've worked frequently with both—I didn't feel that same sense of skepticism from them. At least not while they were there with me in the houses.

Whether we're aware of them or not, ghosts have always been among us—and they have been a part of my life since my early childhood. These days, I do believe that the mainstream is becoming much more accepting of the reality of earthbound spirits. People who sense that something isn't right in their homes or business search out my Web site and seek my advice. Although I have never advertised what I do, word of mouth has resulted in countless calls coming in on the six phone lines installed in my house. (My husband has nicknamed them "the weird lines.")

It was word of mouth, in fact, that led me to my job as consultant for *Ghost Whisperer*. About four years ago, I received a call from a woman who introduced herself as James Van Praagh's assistant. Of course I knew who James was: He is one of the best-known mediums today. He doesn't talk to, or see, earthbound spirits as I can. Instead, he is able to communicate with spirits who have crossed over, or gone into the white Light. I knew of his books and his daily television show, and I told Kelly that I'd be delighted to speak to him.

I was flattered to think James had even heard of me. At the time, I had self-published a few books, and articles about me would sometimes appear in the local Cleveland papers—usually around Halloween—but the majority of calls I got were from people who had heard firsthand from a relative or friend about how I had helped them rid their home of a ghost or had attended the viewing before a funeral to help them finalize family plans or straighten out misunderstandings.

Homeowners in Oklahoma had called James about their house being haunted, and he invited me to visit the house with him for his TV show. I was happy to help out. When James and I arrived at the house, the homeowners were cordial, if slightly overwhelmed by the number of camera operators and technicians and equipment operators who had crowded into their nicely decorated ranch home. Before we began filming, I took a walk through the house. I'd done enough television to know that dead airtime is not a good thing. And if a spirit isn't going to want to talk to me or is going to be stingy with information, it helps me to know this in advance.

There were a bonanza of ghosts in this house—five in all—which was not surprising given the troubles the family was reporting: The checkbook would constantly go missing; the two boys in the family suffered from respiratory infections and were frequent nighttime visitors to their parents' room, claiming they just couldn't sleep in their room. The mother was sick of finding her kids' expensive toys broken, each boy claiming he had nothing to do with it—he'd just found them that way.

So as the cameras rolled, I did what I usually do. I asked the ghosts their names and how old they were and where they were from. The parents wanted to know more about the ghost that they had always assumed was the imaginary friend of their younger child. The older boy just hung back at the edge of the group, but I could tell he was worried about something.

While they are young, most children have a remarkable ability to see or sense the spirits who surround them. For some, these ghosts—especially if they are the spirits of children themselves—become the "imaginary friends" who break toys or cause loud one-sided conversations. For other children, these not-real people cause very real unease.

"The man in the plaid flannel shirt who shows up in your bedroom sometimes really scares you, doesn't he?" I spoke directly to the older boy, who nodded and burst into tears. I glared at the spirit in question, a young man with a bad mullet hairdo and a flannel shirt. He stared back with a surly expression, just like the bully he was. But most ghosts, no matter how mean-spirited, don't intimidate me at all.

I turned back to the boy. "Don't worry," I said. "I promise he'll be gone after today."

True to my word, I made the white Light, and one by one all the spirits departed from the house, including the ghost of a next-door neighbor who had wandered over, curious to see what was going on with all the lights and crowds, but only too happy to be able to take advantage of the chance to leave his earthbound existence.

After we had done this shoot together, I came to consider James a good friend. He knows many, many people from all walks of life and frequently calls me to say he has a friend or acquaintance or business associate who might need my services. Because

James lives on the West Coast, whenever I was out in that area he invited me along to dinners or cocktail parties. Inevitably there was a ghost or two on the premises. Earthbound spirits are pure energy and need energy to subsist. And believe me, what with actors, directors, writers, and other types of creative people, Hollywood has energy to spare.

The idea that became *Ghost Whisperer* came out of one of these parties. James had invited me to join him and a few friends for dinner. The host and hostess—a studio executive and her husband, a television writer—were warm and welcoming. They lived in a glamorous old house that had once belonged to the cowboy actor Tom Mix. Tom wasn't there that night, but there were several other ghostly dinner guests joining us. The food looked wonderful, but luckily I wasn't hungry. I learned long ago that if I'm invited to a dinner party, it's wise to eat my dinner at home before I go out. Once I'm at the table, I'm always so busy answering questions that I almost never get a chance to eat what the host is serving!

This time was no exception. I told the hosts about the frustrated writer ghost who spent his time with the husband in his study.

"This explains your trouble in deciding where to set the story you're working on," I told him. "You thought you should set it in the mountains. The ghost thinks it would work better at the beach."

The man and his wife stared at me openmouthed.

"There's another spirit here, too," I told them. "She came with the antique bureau you got recently—the one with a mirror on it."

The woman frowned. "We don't have an antique bureau in the house."

"It's downstairs," the ghost told me.

"She says it's downstairs," I repeated.

The other couple at the table gasped. "We live downstairs,"

the woman explained. "And we recently bought an old bedroom set at an auction. It has a bureau with a mirror."

I wasn't surprised. Ghosts often attach themselves to material possessions such as important pieces of furniture, jewelry, or vintage cars. I guess they feel that if they can't take it with them, they'll just make sure they don't lose sight of it.

The rest of the night passed quickly, with me trying to steal bites of my dessert in between answering more questions about the spirits in the house with us, and about others I have encountered in my line of work. As James and I were leaving, our hosts walked us to the door.

"Your experiences are amazing," the man said. "They'd make a great TV show."

I didn't really think that much about it. Since I'd been in California, lots of people had told me that my ghost stories would make great TV. But nothing had come of it. So when James called me a few weeks later and told me to get myself right down to the Starbucks at the corner of Hollywood and Vine to meet with a producer named John Gray, I didn't have any big expectations.

When I got to the Starbucks, I realized that I had forgotten to ask James what John Gray looked like. All I knew was that he was from New York, not California. My husband, Ted, had come with me to the meeting, and when I spied the tall, thin man in a black windbreaker pacing outside the coffeehouse door, I sent Ted out to see if I had indeed picked out the New Yorker from the California coffee crowd.

In fact I had, and our meeting lasted three hours. I simply told John what I did as he asked question after question. The first thing he asked me was where we could go to find some ghosts.

"We don't have to go anywhere," I said. "There are spirits here right now."

"Right here in Starbucks," he said, looking around.

"Right here in Starbucks," I confirmed.

I told him about the ghost of an older woman I'd been watching while waiting for him to arrive. She'd been standing very close to a handsome young man who resembled her, and who I suspected was her son. Whenever an attractive woman came through the door, Mom would do everything she could to get her son to glance in that direction. Of course, he was paying more attention to his BlackBerry than anything else, and her frustration mounted each time another potential daughter-in-law left without notice.

Then I told him about the ghost of an older Mexican man who was standing behind the counter with the barista. He was touching all the dials on the espresso machine and generally wreaking havoc until the poor kid who was working at filling the coffee orders was at his wit's end.

John just listened to me talk and stared at the kid as he dropped cups, splashed steamed milk, and spilled espressos. If you watched the pilot episode of *Ghost Whisperer*, you'll remember that both these ghosts were worked into the script.

I left the meeting thinking how much I had enjoyed talking to John. I never expected the call I got a few hours later, though. It was James, telling me that John was interested in doing a show about a woman who could see and talk to ghosts.

Once I began traveling out to California fairly regularly to work with the writers on the show, it became customary for me to spend time on some of the sets and soundstages. Ghosts can be very disruptive, particularly to electrical equipment and light-bulbs. It takes only one expensive piece of equipment to malfunction or one actor to get showered with glass from an exploding light for the people on set to ask me to clear out the lingering spirits who just can't seem to accept that their final credits have rolled.

It's easy for anyone to get a bit starstruck after spending time in Hollywood: Everywhere you look, you spot familiar faces from film or television. Before you know it, you're hoping to run into your favorite celebrities at the corner Starbucks. I was no different when it came to Hollywood spirits. Each time I checked out a studio lot, a soundstage, or a prop storage area, I hoped I might run into a big star, like James Dean or Elvis. But for the most part, I met a lot of B-list starlets and old technical guys who just hadn't been able to bring themselves to leave the business they loved.

Being affiliated with *Ghost Whisperer* has certainly changed my circumstances. It's raised my profile and increased both believers and detractors. I'm sure it's no surprise to find out that I'm a big fan of the show. The character of Melinda Gordon is glamorous yet grounded, and the spirits she encounters are complex and interesting. So it may be a disappointment to hear that I don't find my own life as a paranormal investigator quite as dramatic. I see and talk to ghosts nearly every day, and if each encounter were so steeped in drama, frankly, I'd be exhausted. The truth is, a good TV show is scary and sexy and highly theatrical. It's entertainment, not real life, after all.

Seeing and talking to spirits is a part of my real life and something I've done since I was a child. As far as earthbound spirits are concerned, I have an awful lot of experience. One of the producers on the show, exasperated after listening to me complain about the way one of the actors looked in ghostly makeup, suggested that maybe I should write a book to make sure that people know what's true and what isn't.

Born out of exasperation or not, it was actually a pretty good idea. Blood may not drip down the walls, and the attic may not be host to swarms of buzzing flies, but the reality is that ghosts are all around us. And more often than not, the truth is much more intriguing than the fiction. This book tells my real-life story—from early-childhood years spent attending funerals with my grandmother to my current day job as a paranormal investigator. I'll share stories of working with law enforcement, celebrities, sports teams, and completely average folks, all of whom have been amazed at what I can tell them from talking to the spirits who surround them. I'll discuss the myths and realities of earthbound spirits. And I'll tell you how you can become more attuned to them and protect yourself, your home, or your family from unwanted visitors.

Since I've been working as a paranormal investigator, I've watched the fascination with earthbound spirits increase and become mainstream. But along with all the interest, there's also a lot of misinformation out there. There are things everyone should know about dealing with ghosts, and I'm prepared to tell you about them. In the chapters that follow, I'll share remarkable stories from my career, as well as practical advice that will help you peacefully coexist with the earthbound spirits who cross your path every day.

1

MY STORY

Discovering a Gift

I HAD HEARD my grandmother tell the story so often that by the time I was grown, it was as if I had my own true memory of the moment I saw my first earthbound spirit. I was just a few months older than two and had been left to stay with Nonna and Nonno (grandmother and grandfather) while my mother was off at the hospital giving birth to my sister. Now, in those days, having a baby wasn't a drive-through event the way it is today. My mother would be in the hospital for nearly a week, and it wasn't an option for a father to take time off from work when a baby arrived. So I was dropped off at my grandparents' house for an extended visit while my parents went off to the hospital.

I'm sure I was happy about staying with my grandparents. As the firstborn grandchild, I occupied a special place in my grandmother's world. My maternal grandparents were both born in the small village of Caramanica, Italy, near Rome. The women in my grandmother's family were known and respected for their special abilities. My grandmother, her mother, her mother's mother—and so on—were sought out by villagers suffering from curses such as the *malocchio*, evil eye. My grandmother grew up proud of her ability to lift curses. When she and her husband emigrated to the

Cleveland area, they happily settled in a neighborhood of Italian immigrants, many from the same or surrounding towns.

In this new country, my grandmother's abilities became even more important. Transatlantic news traveled slowly, and when my grandparents first arrived in Cleveland, it could be weeks before any kind of tidings arrived from the Old Country. But my grandmother didn't need to rely on the Caramanica-to-Cleveland mail.

Periodically she would announce that she was experiencing "that feeling." "*Ho pelle de oca,*" she'd exclaim, rubbing her arms and showing me the goose bumps. She knew what the eerie sensation meant: That night she would dream of someone, often someone from her hometown or a nearby village. Then she would know that another *paesano*, countryman, had died.

My grandmother would wake the next morning, and in properly somber fashion, head to the house of whatever relatives were in the neighborhood. Solemnly she'd deliver the news: "Antonio [or Angela or Luigi or Giovanni] has died." And sure enough, three or four weeks later the letter would arrive from Italy, full of the sad details. My grandmother was famous in her neighborhood. "Maria has the gift," the neighbors would announce proudly.

The way my grandmother always told me the story was that early in the week while I was staying with her and Grandfather, she had one of her dreams. The next morning, she took me along with her when she went over to the neighbor's house. There, over cups of espresso and biscotti, they discussed the sad death of *compa* Dominic while I played on the kitchen floor with an old teapot and cups.

That day, after my nap, Grandmother put me in the sunroom and went about her chores. As she passed by the sunroom, she heard me happily babbling away in Italian. This was not so unusual in and of itself: Although my parents spoke mainly English in our house, my grandparents knew very little, so in their home Italian was the language we all spoke.

She stuck her head around the doorway and saw me. I was sitting on the floor, facing a corner of the room. I was waving my hands and nodding as if I were conversing with someone.

"Mary Ann, who are you talking to?" she asked.

"He says he is *paesano*," I replied.

"Where is he?" she asked.

I pointed to the empty corner.

At first, Grandmother admitted, she thought that I was just imitating the conversation I had overheard that morning at the neighbor's house.

She began to ask me questions. "What does the *paesan'* look like? Where is his home? How did he get here? What has happened to him?"

As I answered each of her questions, my grandmother came to believe that I was talking to the man who had just died. No two-year-old could have made up the answers to the questions she was asking. By the end of her interrogation, my grandmother knew that I was not simply playacting a scene I had witnessed earlier. She knew that I was speaking to a ghost.

My grandmother wasn't worried. In fact, she couldn't have been happier. Her daughter—my mother—did not have the gift, and my grandmother had worried about who would carry on for her family. Now, to her great relief, though it had skipped a generation, her family gift for interacting with spirits had been passed along.

From the time I was four years old, my grandmother began taking me with her to funerals in the neighborhood. It was the early 1950s, and in the ethnic neighborhoods of Cleveland, Italian families stuck to the ways of the Old Country. My first impressions of funerals consisted mainly of large, garlicky women clasping me to their generous bosoms or pinching my cheeks while exclaiming to my grandmother, "The *bambina* has the gift. Ah, Maria, you must be so proud!"

My grandmother, who always turned out for the occasion with her wiry black hair freshly finger-waved and held in place by "diamond" bobby pins and her lips and nails gleaming with her signature Revlon Fifth Avenue Red, would modestly accept compliments on my behalf, beaming with pride and importance. Then, prompted by the family members and my grandmother, I'd inform the stunned-looking man or woman who was standing at the foot of the casket that I had some questions and would then relay his or her answers to the mourners who were gathered.

When I was going on all these "outings" with my grandmother, I don't think my parents ever knew exactly what I was doing. By now, with four small girls at home, my mother was probably mostly grateful that my grandmother wanted to spend so much time with me. What I'm even more certain of, however, is that the idea of actually questioning my grandmother—the undisputed matriarch of the family—never crossed my parents' minds! I don't think it ever crossed my grandmother's mind to tell her daughter, my mother, who didn't have the gift, why she was spending so much time taking me on outings. Maybe she was disappointed that her abilities had skipped a generation; maybe she thought her own daughter would disapprove—I never found out for sure. But I'm certain neither of my parents knew what I could do when I was a child.

When I spoke to my father's ghost at his funeral, he was completely shocked! He recovered fairly well, though, muttering something along the lines of "Your mother's family was always rather exotic," and letting it go. After that, I decided there was no real reason to tell my mother.

Of course, once I married Ted, I had two more parents to deal with. I did finally tell my mother-in-law what I was doing most afternoons when I left the house. After all, she was living with us. She never questioned what I told her, although I could tell she was skeptical. When she died, I reminded her ghost that I had always said I'd be the last person she ever talked to. I guess that took care of her skepticism.

My own first *real* memory of really talking to a spirit is from when I was about seven. The experience was unique to me for a couple of reasons. For one thing, it was the first time I'd seen a young ghost. And second, the encounter led to my first deeper understanding of how spirits became earthbound.

It was in the last few weeks of summer, right before I was about to start second grade, when my grandmother announced to my parents that she was taking me to New York for a visit.

"*Comare* Gina is having some problems in her house," my grandmother told me as we arrived at the airport. I was so excited about taking my first plane trip that I didn't even think to ask about what kind of problems—or why I should care. If I'd been paying more attention, I probably would have realized that this visit wasn't going to be like a trip to the funeral home.

Gina lived in an elegant town house on a tree-lined street in New York City. We entered into a dim foyer paneled with dark wood, and I waited patiently while my grandmother and Gina exchanged greetings and gossip. Gina led us into the parlor, where my grandmother turned her attention to me. "Is anyone here?" she asked.

I nodded. But before my grandmother or Gina could ask me any questions, I blurted out, "Oh, Grandma! She's so pretty!"

It made such an impression on me that I can still clearly re-member the spirit who was standing in the parlor with us that day. She was a slim, pale woman, maybe twenty years old, with dark hair that hung almost to her waist. She was wearing what I now know was a peignoir set (but to my seven-year-old eyes looked like a very bare evening gown and jacket). Her silky white gown floated down to her bare feet, and her long fingers were nearly hidden by the marabou-feather cuffs of her robe.

I really didn't know what to think. The men and women I had talked to at the funeral homes were old. They had lived long and full lives. It had been time for them to die. But this pretty ghost seemed lost and sad.

My grandmother and *comare* Gina asked several questions, and I relayed the ghost's answers. Ghosts are perfectly capable of hearing what everyone is saying. And when they talk to me I just sort of hear their answers in my head. Furthermore, when I talk to spirits, I don't speak aloud, it's more of an internal dialogue. As I grew older, I was particularly grateful for this, as I often got more information from the ghost than I wanted to share with the people in the room—remember, ghosts can observe the people they're living with at any time! And it came in handy to be able to offer silent comments if the things people were saying upset the spirit in the room with them.

From the young woman ghost's answers, it became clear to everyone that she had, in fact, been causing problems in the house. Gina had been suffering from terrible headaches. Her important jewelry was always being misplaced. She was convinced that she had a curse on her, which was why she had summoned my grandmother. My grandmother suspected that the problem might be a ghost, which was why she had brought me along. Once Gina was satisfied that the young woman's ghost was the source of her problems, my grandmother was perfectly clear on what had to happen next.

"Okay, Mary Ann, you tell her to leave now," Grandmother said.

I had done this before on occasion. We would be at a funeral, or occasionally at the grave site, and my grandmother would whisper to me, "Tell them they should leave now." And I would turn to the ghost watching the ceremony and say, "Grandma says you need to go."

And each time the ghost would turn and walk into the glow of a white Light that was always hovering nearby. I would watch them walk into the Light; then the Light faded, and the ghost was gone. My grandmother would study my face, then ask, "So they're gone?" And I'd tell her that they were, and home we'd go.

As pretty as this lady ghost was, and as much as I wanted to ask her why she seemed so sad, I knew better than to question my grandmother. And so I told the ghost that she needed to leave.

"I want to leave," she said, bursting into tears. "But I want to be sure I go to heaven."

This made a big impression on me. I was about to begin second grade. It was the year I would make my First Communion, and I could understand how going to heaven would be a high priority. I'd been thinking about making my First Communion all summer and was trying to be extra good and holy, so I felt pretty confident when I told her, "Okay, then just go to a church."

The ghost smiled sadly. "I've tried that," she said. "I've gone to churches all over the city. But I can't get to heaven from there."

My grandmother and Gina were watching me intently. "Is she gone yet?" Gina whispered to my grandmother.

"Mary Ann, has she gone?" my grandmother asked.

"No, Grandma, she says she wants to be sure to go to heaven," I said helplessly.

"Well, tell her to go to a church, then," my grandmother said, with a note of impatience in her voice.

I knew better than to argue with my grandmother when her voice had that tone. Besides, when Gina heard that the ghost wasn't leaving, she began to sob, pulling a big white hankie from the pocket of her sundress. I looked from *comare* Gina to my grandmother to the ghost.

"You *have to* go," I said. "You're making everyone upset."

The ghost nodded, and as she passed me, she raised her hand as if to stroke my cheek. She walked out of the parlor and into the dark foyer, toward the front door. And then she was gone.

"She's not here anymore," I told my grandmother and *comare* Gina.

Gina hugged my grandmother and then me, all the while exclaiming: "How proud you must be, Maria, to have a grandchild with such a gift!"

My grandmother beamed and nodded. This part, at least, was just like at the funerals.

On the flight home, I couldn't stop thinking about the sad, beautiful ghost. There was something different about her. Not just that she was young and pretty, but something else. Suddenly I realized what it was.

"Grandma," I said, pulling at her arm. "I think I know why the lady was so sad."

I explained how all the other spirits I saw always had a bright white Light near them. I explained, too, that whenever I told them it was time to go, they would walk toward that Light, then into the Light until I couldn't see them anymore, and they'd be gone.

"The pretty lady didn't have any Light with her," I said. "I think that was why she was so sad."

My grandmother was quiet. I knew she had listened intently, and I didn't mind that she didn't have anything to say. In fact, I can remember feeling pretty pleased with myself for figuring out what had been bothering the sad spirit.

Two weeks later, however, my grandmother called me outside at the end of the day. She told me to look toward the setting sun. Squinting, I did as I was told.

"Is the Light around the spirits as bright as that?" she asked.

"It's brighter, but it doesn't hurt my eyes," I told her.

My grandmother gestured toward the wall of the garage. "Make the Light there," she told me.

I had no idea what she was talking about. But again, the rule was, when Grandma asked me to do something, I didn't ask questions. And so I stared at the side of the garage, trying to visualize the bright glow. I can't tell you exactly how it happened, but suddenly I saw a flicker of light against the evening shadows. I willed it to become brighter, and it did.

"I did it," I said, turning to my grandmother. When I looked back at the garage, the Light was gone.

Eventually, with practice, I could make the Light appear at will, and over the years I have learned how to make it bigger, brighter, and steadier. The more I made the Light, the more I learned how to keep it present for longer periods of time, and the more I appreciated and understood the power that it held.

From the first time I made the Light, and every time I made it after that, it was purely a matter of visualizing. I don't experience any particular sensations as I make the Light—no tiredness, no headaches, no feelings of warmth or cold. I simply see it. It's easier for me to make the Light against a solid surface such as a wall or a floor or a tree, or even the ground.

These years were a time when I really began to understand what I was able to do. And I believe this knowledge came at a critical point. From when I was seven to around eight or so—the age that experts call "the age of reason" and the church calls "the age of discretion"—my grandmother took special care to reinforce that although my gift for talking to spirits was special, in every other way I was simply a normal girl. She never told me that the spirits I saw were figments of my imagination or that I was too old to be talking to people whom no one else could see. To this day, I believe her positive encouragement nurtured my gift.

Of course, I also learned the valuable lesson that not everyone was as open to and understanding of the spirit world as my grandmother. When I kept seeing a menacing male spirit walking behind my friend Lizzie, I decided it only made sense to tell my teacher, Sister Mary. After all, as we prepared to make our First Holy Communion during second grade, the nuns talked frequently about the Holy Ghost. Surely if they couldn't see what I could, then at least they believed in it, I reasoned.

"Sister, there's a bad man following Lizzie," I told her.

Sister Mary glanced toward Lizzie, and, obviously seeing no one, turned back to me. "It's her guardian angel," she said.

Now, I had seen pictures of guardian angels in picture books, on the walls of my classroom, and even in framed photos in houses, and they were beautiful creatures, with golden halos and snow-white wings. The swarthy, dark-haired man who slouched around the playground looked nothing like them at all. But I wasn't going to argue with a nun, so I let it go.

A few weeks later, when he appeared again, I felt like I had to speak up.

"Sister Mary, that man is standing behind Lizzie again, and I don't think he is an angel," I announced.

Sister Mary took me by the shoulders. "Mary Ann, you stop this right now! If I hear any more from you, I'll send you to the priest. You're not going to make your First Communion if you continue to talk like this."

When I went home that afternoon, I told my grandmother what had happened. "It is better not to tell people unless they ask," she said. "People can be frightened by things they don't understand; it can make them angry. Let people ask you."

To this day, I don't volunteer information. I notice spirits all the time, and over the years I have been privy to more private and personal information than I care to know. But that early lesson has stuck with me: Unless someone asks me a direct question, I don't share what I see or hear.

Of course, as I grew from a young child who was flattered by my grandmother's attention and praise, into a typical teenager, I naturally rebelled against my ability. It seemed less a gift than an incredibly weird impediment to my social life. I had better things to do on a Friday night than to go hang out with my grandmother at a funeral parlor for a viewing. So when I was around fourteen or fifteen years old, I made a conscious decision that I wasn't going to see spirits anymore.

Looking back on this period, I realize that it was a typical teenage rebellion against the living, not the dead. After all, if I told my grandmother that I just didn't see ghosts anymore, how could she prove me wrong? Of course the flaw in this logic was my assumption that my grandmother couldn't immediately tell when I was lying.

When I first hatched this plan to get out of going to funerals every weekend, we'd be at someone's viewing and my grandmother would prompt me: "Mary Ann, is anyone here?"

"Nope, Grandma. Sorry. I don't see anyone," I'd say, desperately avoiding eye contact.

My grandmother would reach out, grasp my chin in her hands, and force me to meet her narrowed gaze. "Is that the truth?" she'd ask—her dark eyes looking right through me.

"Oh, fine." I'd sigh, rolling my eyes. "He's right over there by the flowers arranged like a horseshoe."

"*Bene*. Good," she'd say with satisfaction as she dragged me off to speak to the grieving widow.

My next move was to try to avoid my grandmother whenever possible, telling her that I was busy with school or friends or boys. But even that technique was unsuccessful. She was a willful woman, and I really wasn't cut out for the life of a rebel.

Though this phase of denial didn't last long, it was important in that it taught me how to tune out the ghosts who are present nearly everywhere I go. To me, earthbound spirits look just like living people—though if I stare at them and squint really hard, I can see through them. But at first glance, I just see a person. Maybe it's a man with dark hair and brown eyes wearing a tan sport coat and plaid tie. He might even be smoking a cigarette— at least if he's from a certain generation. An outfit can actually be a pretty good tip-off that I'm seeing an earthbound spirit. I mean, someone who died in the 1940s is probably going to be wearing something that sticks out in a crowd.

Pretty much anyplace I go has a few earthbound spirits hanging around, but I've learned to ignore them if I haven't been asked to talk to them; I've learned not to stare. Just as I can sense if someone is watching me—and once I'm aware, glance around until I locate the person who is staring—so, too, can earthbound spirits become aware of my gaze. And if I stare, it doesn't take long before they notice that I'm watching them.

In any case, my self-imposed retirement didn't last long. Soon my grandmother was calling me regularly and insisting that I go with her to the calling hours at *compa* Aldo's viewing, and off I would go, to help settle family affairs and bask in my grandmother's proud smiles.

Besides, my social life was going just fine, thank you very much.

I was a sixteen-year-old high school sophomore when I first met Ted. He was a good friend of my boyfriend at the time, and we often double-dated. To tell you the truth, he and I didn't get along too well at first. I went to Catholic school, and though Ted was Catholic, his parents had sent him to the local public school. Back in those days, the kids at the Catholic schools and those at the public schools usually didn't mix socially.

Ted was a year older than I was, and after he graduated he joined the navy and went off to training. I really didn't give him much more thought until he stopped by to visit Frank while he was on leave. By this time I was eighteen, Frank and I had broken up, and what can I say? I'm apparently a sucker for a tall handsome guy in a uniform. Ted and I began a long-distance romance, writing each other lengthy letters while he was in Vietnam.

When he came home from active duty, our romance continued. We became engaged and planned to marry in late February. Two weeks before our wedding date, Ted's reserve unit was put on standby to head out to Cuba. When Ted called me at work to tell me he might have to leave immediately, I sprang into action, calling the priest at our local parish and pleading with him to marry us that night.

He did: We were wed on a February night in 1968. A year later, our first child was born. I still hadn't told Ted about what I could do. I was enjoying being a new wife and figured there was no need to freak out my husband by telling him what I was doing with my grandmother when she asked me to attend a funeral with her. He probably thought I was just a devoted granddaughter.

I wanted to eventually tell Ted what I could do, but I was waiting for the right time. Even though we were now married, much of our courtship had been long distance, and in some ways we were still getting to know each other. Under those circumstances, *Oh, by the way, honey, I've been meaning to tell you that I can see and talk to ghosts* really didn't roll off the tongue. So time passed, as I waited for a signal that the moment was right to share my secret.

As a young couple with a baby, back in the late 1960s, we didn't have a lot of money to spend on going out on the weekends, so more often than not we'd end up playing cards with another couple Ted knew from work. Our babies were the same age, and on Saturday nights, while the girls shared a crib, the four of us would sit around the dining room table—at our house or theirs—and play cards. Of course I preferred it when we played at our house. Mike and Joanie's house had a female ghost whom I found very distracting. Joanie never mentioned anything to me about thinking her house was haunted, and I was sticking to my rule about not saying anything unless asked, so I did my best to ignore the ghost whenever I was at the house.

Late one Saturday night, we were at Mike and Joanie's playing pinochle. Suddenly there was a tremendous crash in the kitchen. It sounded as if every dish had flown out of the cupboard and smashed in the sink. Ted and Mike jumped up from the table and rushed into the kitchen. Joanie sat calmly at the table, looking at her cards. The guys were in the kitchen, out of our sight and silent.

Then Joanie called out to Mike: "So *now* do you believe me? I told you we have a ghost in this house."

She turned to me. "It turns on the dryer, it turns off the washer, it messes with the thermostat for the heat," she said. "The other day, it even turned on the musical mobile hanging over the baby's bed. And during her nap, too!"

The men returned to the room looking completely bewildered. I just kept my head down and my eyes on my cards. This wasn't how I wanted to let my new husband know that I could actually see the ghost wreaking havoc in the kitchen.

Now, being pretty typical guys, Mike and Ted weren't going to admit that the noise in the kitchen didn't have a logical explanation. After much discussion between them, Mike announced with confidence that he was sure that the noise we had heard was a sonic boom. It was obvious: A late-night flyover had been responsible for rattling all the dishes. Satisfied with his explanation, Mike dealt a new hand of cards while Joanie rolled her eyes. I wondered uncomfortably how much longer I could ignore the spirit who had joined us in the dining room and was having a good laugh at all the speculation.

Later that evening, as we were driving home with the baby sleeping in the back of the car, I asked Ted, "So do you really think that was a sonic boom?"

Ted admitted that it seemed unlikely, but since it was Mike's house, he thought he'd be polite and agree.

As casually as I could, I asked my next question: "Did you hear what Joanie was saying about a ghost?"

"I did hear that," he said.

"What do you think?" I continued. "Do you think there could—maybe—be such things as ghosts?"

Ted thought for a while and then admitted that sure, maybe there could be.

"Have *you* ever seen a ghost?" I persisted.

Ted never had.

"How about your parents? Did they ever think they saw ghosts?"

Ted shook his head. By now he was sneaking sideways glances at me, no doubt wondering why he was suddenly getting the third degree.

I knew it was time to tell him. It was now or never. I took a deep breath and inched my way toward revealing my secret.

"You know how every time my grandma calls me up and tells me I have to go to a funeral with her, I go?"

Ted nodded.

"Do you think that it's a bit strange that I go to all these funerals?" I asked.

Ted admitted to me that, yes, he did think it was odd that

I kept running off with my grandmother, especially to funerals. After all, I was a married woman with a family of my own, and I didn't even know most of the people who had died.

"So tell me," he added, "why do you keep going?"

I looked at him and kept my gaze steady as, barely stopping to take a breath, I blurted out everything. I told him about my grandmother, and the funerals, and the white Light, and the nuns at my grade school, and the ghost in Joanie's kitchen.

And then I told him to stop staring at me and watch the road.

Ted didn't say a word for the rest of the drive. When we got home, he carried our daughter into the house and put her in her crib. I was in the kitchen, setting up the coffeepot for the next morning, when he appeared in the doorway.

He braced a hand on either side of the door and looked straight at me. "Okay," he said. "I'm ready."

"For what?" I asked.

"Go ahead," he said grimly. "Just go ahead and do it."

"Do what?" I asked, truly bewildered.

"Wiggle your nose, or whatever it is you do. I'm ready."

I didn't know whether to cry or laugh. As calmly as I could, I straightened Ted out on what it was I did—and how it didn't resemble Elizabeth Montgomery's character on the television show *Bewitched* in the slightest. Mostly, I reassured him that I was the same person he'd always known; I was just particularly popular at funerals.

He made his peace with my gift pretty quickly. Aside from a few frantic years when he asked if our daughter was talking to earthbound spirits every time she had an imaginary friend (she wasn't, although our younger daughter is able to), our life pretty much picked up and went on much as before. I'll admit that not many husbands would have taken such unusual news in stride. It's just one more thing I love about the guy I married.

A few years later, by the time I was twenty-two, it was quite common for me to be going to funerals on my own. Without my grandmother "managing" my appearance, people felt free to ask me questions. The most common question I was asked was "If you can see ghosts at funerals, can't you see them other places?" When I responded that, yes, I could see spirits outside funeral homes, people began to ask if I would visit their homes. They were sure, they told me, that they had ghosts living in their houses. And often they were right.

I could make the white Light at will, and I felt I was old enough to tell a ghost to leave without needing the imposing personality of my grandmother to back me up, so I began visiting the houses of relatives and friends of the family whom I met at neighborhood funerals. Word of mouth was the most effective way to pass on information in our close-knit neighborhood, and before long I was going to fewer funerals and spending more time traveling to homes where people were living with, and bothered by, earthbound spirits. Just as my grandmother could lift a curse, so could I clear a house of an energy-disrupting spirit.

As the children grew older, our lives changed to meet their needs. We moved to a rural area about an hour south of Cleveland where they could enjoy a more bucolic childhood. Ted changed from working as a mechanic to managing a car dealership. I worked full-time as an animal groomer and enjoyed raising and showing dogs. (And yes, animal spirits can become earthbound just like human spirits.)

As word spread about what I could do, I found that I was getting more and more calls to visit people's houses and rid them of ghosts. It wasn't an easy time. I really felt I had to do my best to get out to every homeowner or businessperson who called me in. Earthbound spirits can wreak havoc in homes and be detrimental to people's health and moods. If someone strongly felt they had a ghost or negative energy in their house, I wanted to do whatever I could to help clear out the spirit and improve the situation.

At the same time, I was a busy working mother of two. Ted and I had also begun welcoming foster babies into our family. So sometimes, I was a busy working mother of three! Then Ted's aging parents moved in with us. After I did a few local radio and newspaper interviews, the calls from people having trouble with earthbound spirits increased. *Overwhelming* doesn't even begin to describe some of the days I had.

So in a way, I was grateful for the hours alone in the car on days when I was called to homes fifty or sixty miles north, toward Cleveland. Usually I tried to minimize my driving, grouping my visits together by location. Still, it was exhausting, and in the back of my mind I knew that something had to give. The solution, when it came, was not one I would have expected.

It was a dreary, gray February day, and I had arranged to visit three homes west of Cleveland. I left in the early morning and arrived at the first house just after breakfast time. The woman who had called had told me that she was quite certain she had a ghost. She had a long list of unexplained occurrences: lights flickering on and off, appliances turning off midcycle, strange bumps and thumps from her heating system. It certainly sounded likely that an earthbound spirit was sharing her residence.

But when I arrived at the small, neat ranch house and took a look around, I could immediately see that there were no spirits present at all, and told the woman so. She was hugely disappointed to find out it wasn't my services she needed, but rather those of a good electrician. I drove on to the next house, where the woman eagerly greeted me and explained that she had heard me speak on the radio. "I've told all my friends that you're coming to get rid of my ghost," she said, looking at me expectantly.

I walked through her house several times. I went from the attic to the basement and even checked the garage that was attached to the house by a breezeway. But once again: nothing. No spirits. And this woman wasn't simply disappointed about it—she was angry with me. "I've told all of my friends that you were going to tell me about my ghosts," she snapped. "Now what am I supposed to say?"

As you might imagine, I was getting a bit frustrated. I felt like telling her that my gift was for making ghosts leave, not appear.

Instead I just got back in my car. After stopping for a fast-food lunch, I arrived at the third and final house. I'm sure you can guess what happened: no ghost.

At the homeowner's insistence, I examined tiny crawl spaces and even a root cellar, but in the end all I could tell her was that she did not have any spirits. This woman, however, was relentless. She had gone to all the trouble of getting me out there, and she wanted a ghost.

"You just need to stay until you find me one," she declared, standing in the middle of her living room, her hands firmly planted on her hips.

"That's ridiculous," I told her as I opened the front door. "I can't summon up a ghost for you."

Livid, the woman followed me out to my car, complaining bitterly the whole way.

I was only too eager to go home. I was frustrated, too. I'd spent the whole day away from my family and my work and I hadn't been of help to anyone, human or spirit. As dusk fell, I began the long drive. About an hour away from home, a freak snow squall blew in out of nowhere and I sat stranded in my car, waiting for it to pass. By the time I got home, it was well after dinner, Ted had already put the kids to bed, and I had decided I was finished with traveling house-to-house to clear out ghosts.

"I'm done," I said to Ted. "I can't do this anymore."

To his credit, Ted, who has never been anything less than supportive of what I do, didn't say a word.

That night, as I lay in bed, exhausted from the day, I added a little PS to my bedtime prayers: "By the way, God, if you want me to keep doing this kind of work, you're going to have to help me come up with Plan B."

For the next two weeks, although I felt guilty every time I received a message from someone who lived more than a short drive away, I didn't go to any houses or funerals outside my own neighborhood. Then one day I picked up the phone when it rang instead of letting the machine get it. The caller said she had heard me on the radio up in the Cleveland area and wondered if I could help her. She believed she had a ghost in her house.

Forgetting my resolve not to travel out of my own neighborhood, I asked the woman what made her think she had a ghost. As she started to explain what was going on, the most extraordinary thing happened. I began to see bright blue peacock feathers. The woman kept talking away, and I was having visions of feathers. I had no idea what was going on. I'm not a psychic; I don't get visions. But I could not stop seeing those feathers. And then, I noticed they were in a blue vase. I couldn't say how I knew exactly. But I knew that this was important information.

The woman paused for a moment and I jumped in. "Do you have peacock feathers in your house?"

The woman said that she did.

"Are they in a blue vase?"

The woman said they were.

As she answered each question, a picture formed clearly in my mind. The feathers were in a vase; the vase was on the hearth of a fireplace. Above the fireplace was an unusual family tree made from photos, literally hanging on a branch. Deciding I just had to go with what was happening, I asked the woman about the mantel and the photos.

"How do you know all this?" the woman wanted to know. "It's a little spooky."

I didn't mention that I was finding it a little weird myself. Instead I told her that I thought I needed to come out to her house to see what was going on. We made an appointment, and when I got to the house, sure enough, there was a ghost there, too. From that phone call on, I've been able to tell, even from the message on my machine, if there is a spirit in the house of the caller.

At first, I thought I was seeing the environment through the *ghost's* eyes. Sometimes I would see a particular part of a room—including any furniture or artwork—as if I were standing right there in the room. Other times, it was as if I were looking through a smudged or foggy window—I could see some details about the

room, but I might not be able to tell if there was a mirror or a
painting over the fireplace. As I grew more familiar with this new
ability, I realized that not only could I see the room, but I could
also see the ghost who was there. I learned to sense if the spirit
was a man or a woman, and for about how long he or she had
been in the house. I can't speak to the spirits this way, or make
them leave, but I can determine, for certain, if there is or isn't a
ghost at any caller's home.

Since Plan B went into effect, I've been able to save miles of
driving and hours of false calls, and concentrate on helping those
people and spirits who really need me. Since that day, I've never
looked back. I asked for something, I received it, and I took it to
mean that I am supposed to keep doing what I do.

Being a paranormal investigator is now a full-time career for
me. I have worked in almost every state, and in many foreign
countries. I have six phone lines for my business coming into the
house, and I keep messages from callers on yellow-lined legal pads.
(I'm up to about eighteen for out-of-state calls and six for local.)
I'm constantly on the phone or on the road. I try to prioritize calls.
If people need me at a funeral, I'll return their call within twenty-
four hours, if I'm in town. Obviously, I can't ask the family to hold
the body for the three or four months it can take for me to get
back to someone calling about a ghost in the house!

I'm well aware of what an odd business I'm in. I walk into
strangers' homes and am often given information that I don't particularly want—or need—to know. And I've become pretty good
at knowing what's important for me to share and what I can just
keep to myself.

There was a particularly delicate situation at a house I was
visiting in Maine. The well-kept, fairly new ranch home had
been suffering from a lot of electrical problems, and the woman
and her husband had been arguing more than usual. I knew from
speaking to the woman that there was a male ghost in their home
who was causing the trouble.

When I arrived, the woman was waiting for me; her husband

was home, but outside working on his Jeep. I asked her if she wanted her husband to come inside so he could ask the ghost questions. She immediately got up and shut the door.

She explained that she needed to ask the ghost something in private, something she didn't want her husband to know she was asking.

I started to get a bit uncomfortable, but the ghost was having a great laugh. I decided I'd try to gently pry. "Are you worried he's having an affair?" I asked.

The woman shook her head, but didn't say anything more.

"Oh, for Pete's sake," the ghost said, still laughing. "She knows her husband is wearing pink lace ladies' underpants."

I couldn't stop myself. I glanced out the window at the legs covered by camouflaged fatigues that were sticking out from under the front of the Jeep. I probably blushed.

"He just told you, didn't he?" the woman demanded. "Well, you should know that I buy them for him. He says that women's panties are just more comfortable. He likes camisoles, too," she added.

I was at a loss. If she already knew this, what kind of secret could she think her husband was keeping from her?

"What I need the ghost to tell me," the woman said urgently, "is if my husband hangs out with other people who do the same thing."

I didn't really want to know myself, but the ghost sighed. "Tell her he doesn't do anything weird except dress in ladies' underwear."

I passed on the information, but the awkward moment still wasn't over.

"You know," the ghost continued thoughtfully, "I sort of know where he's coming from. I mean, I always liked my wife to keep her underwear on when we were . . ." He wiggled his eyebrows suggestively.

By the time I left, the ghost had gone into the Light and the woman was content that her husband simply preferred silk and lace to boxers. I felt like Dr. Ruth or something.

In fact, a lot of the time I do feel like a counselor to both the living and the dead. I help spirits come to peace with their decision to leave—and the living often seem to need reassurance as well.

Over the past fifty years, my ability to talk to earthbound spirits has gone from a secret I shared with my grandmother; to a strange gift acknowledged, but not always accepted, by family, friends, and strangers; to a skill that people want to learn about at workshops and in interviews; to a career that helped inspire a television series.

It seems a natural progression to write this book. As I get busier and see more clients, I realize that people *think* they know a lot about ghosts—but really what they have is a lot of misinformation. Still, I believe that most people can become more sensitive to the spirit world and its connection with ours.

For instance, it occurred to me one day as Ted drove me to a house—where I would meet with the homeowners and clear out a spirit while Ted sat in the car and read a novel—how receptive he has become to the world of earthbound spirits that I am so in tune with. Maybe it's because he has lived with me for thirty-nine years, but when he ran the car dealership and sensed that, for instance, there was a spirit attached to the vehicle he'd just picked up at an auction, he was right nearly every time. And many of the people who call me to ask if they have ghosts because they have been having specific problems are correct as well. They have sensed that something is disrupting the physical or mental energy around them, and have not been afraid to trust that sense.

In the chapters that follow, I'll share with you the knowledge I have gained from more than fifty years of communicating with earthbound spirits. If you have an open mind and a willingness to trust your instincts, I hope that you will gain a deeper understanding of the world of spirits that, for me, has always coexisted with ordinary, everyday life.

PART II

Understanding Earthbound Spirits

2

THE TRUTH ABOUT GHOSTS

Separating Fact from Fiction

IF YOU watch popular television shows like *Medium* and *Ghost Whisperer*, or have seen feature films such as *Ghost*, *The Amityville Horror*, *Stir of Echoes*, *The Sixth Sense*, or *What Lies Beneath*, you are probably aware that earthbound spirits and vindictive ghosts are Hollywood staples for hair-raising entertainment. Of course, since I really do "see dead people . . . all the time," my daily experiences are not always as dramatic as those portrayed on the large or small screen.

Sometimes I sense that people feel let down that having me come and talk to the ghost in their house just isn't as exciting as they thought it might be. They'll ask me to tell the ghost to do this thing or that. And when the ghost simply refuses to perform party tricks on command, some homeowners get downright disappointed with me! They don't understand just how mundane a conversation with that earthbound spirit can be. From my perspective, encountering, talking to, and releasing earthbound spirits is all in a day's work. For me, an encounter with a ghost isn't like a scene from a Hollywood blockbuster. I don't know how I'd be able to carry on a normal life if it were.

Today, in all forms of media, stories involving the living

interacting with the spirit world are increasingly popular, and as a result I've noticed that there's a ton of misinformation out there—behaviors, characteristics, or powers wrongly attributed to earthbound spirits—that people take as true.

Most people who contact me *do* have earthbound spirits in their homes, or have some type of negative energy attached to them. Usually when folks tell me they think there's a ghost nearby, they aren't able to pinpoint a single specific factor causing them to seek my help. More often than not, they've heard me talk on television or the radio about the types of problems that earthbound spirits can cause, and recognize *exactly* the kinds of problems they are currently having themselves. When I confirm for these people that ghosts are indeed around them, they usually say, "Well, I just thought there was something not quite right in the house."

Other folks are completely convinced that they're hosting an earthbound spirit and simply don't believe me when I tell them that their houses are clear. These are the people who will argue endlessly with me: "But I know I have a ghost here because my house has cold spots/I hear chains rattling/I live near a cemetery/there are flies in the attic/my house is built on an old burial ground."

In my fifty-plus years of seeing and communicating with earthbound spirits, I have adopted the philosophy *Never say never*. I don't mind admitting that I may someday come upon spirits able to influence the environment in one of these specific ways. Maybe someday I will meet ghosts wrapped in chains who drag them along the floor and make rattling sounds when they walk. But so far in my experience, having flies in your attic doesn't mean your house is haunted. It probably means you have holes in your window screens.

I can understand why people want to blame their problems on ghosts. It's a simple explanation. They expect that if they call me, I'll come take away the negative energy and remove the earthbound spirit. And in fact, when the problem is related to an earthbound spirit, the solution *is* just that simple. But that's not always the case.

The bottom line is: Sometimes, bad things happen to good people. You cannot blame everything that goes wrong in your life on ghosts. The people who do this are the people I feel bad for. I wonder: What did they do in their past life that they are so miserable in this one? But as much as I'd like to, if there's no spirit or negative energy around these folks, there's really nothing I can do to help. And even when I *can* make a difference, clearing out an earthbound spirit or negative energy doesn't mean the homeowners will go out and win the lottery the next day. All that clearing a house does is give you a level playing field so that you are not held back by bad energies or earthbound spirits.

Earthbound Spirits and Physical Presence

Ghosts Do Not Draw Energy from Your TV or Other Electrical Devices

Many people who do have ghosts in their house report temperamental electronic devices: computers that crash, TVs or cell phones plagued by static, or flickering lights. While these mechanical disruptions can be evidence of the presence of an earthbound spirit, the fact that your lights flicker does not mean a ghost is siphoning your electrical current for the energy he or she needs to survive.

Ghosts do need energy, of course, because they consist of pure energy. They have no physical body, they don't eat, they don't sleep, but they need energy to survive. But not mechanical energy, like the electrical current that powers your computer. The energy ghosts seek out does not have a material form or substance. It is metaphysical. Consider this: People have constant currents of both physical and emotional energy. Your physical energy can be measured by tests such as CAT scans, or MRIs, or using sensors. Your emotional energy, however, is a bit harder to quantify. But it is every bit as real as—and often has a direct effect on—your physical energy. Emotional changes cause your body to react. Think about when a person gets angry, for instance: His blood pressure goes up, his heart rate increases, his whole energy changes.

How many times have you described yourself or someone else as "having a low-energy day"? Or explained your feeling of unease about a stranger by saying she had "negative energy"? Or complimented someone on having a "high-energy" personality? This kind of emotional energy is also easily transferable. You may feel sad and exhausted after a funeral where you spent your time talking with many of the mourners. Or you may feel energized after seeing a funny or exciting movie. Once you understand the concept of the energy fields that we all carry with us, you can begin to understand what kinds of people and situations are the most likely to attract earthbound spirits.

Now to go back to the flickering lights, crashing computer, and static-filled cell phone for a moment: If a ghost is pure energy and stands next to something that is using another source of energy, doesn't it make sense that one might interfere with the other in some way—maybe at the source of the energy, in the wiring, or with the machine itself? It's not too difficult for earthbound spirits to realize that if they stand next to your computer, it's likely to crash. And the same ghosts quickly notice that when your computer crashes, you go ballistic. And when you go ballistic, the ghosts get a very satisfying surge of energy. How often do you think these ghosts will stand next to your computer when you're working hoping for a quick energy fix?

Ghosts Cannot Draw Energy from Other Earthbound Spirits

Ghosts need the emotional, metaphysical energy generated by the living to fuel their existence; they cannot draw this energy from other earthbound spirits. In fact, when one ghost comes into a room to find that another ghost is already there, generally one or the other of them will turn around and leave. If you have multiple spirits in your home, you can be sure that they all gravitate to different areas of the house. They don't sit around playing cards with one another all day. The exception to this is if the ghosts are gathered in high-energy places such as theaters, where a crowd of the living generates more than enough energy.

When ghosts cannot get enough energy, they become lethargic and generally head off in search of a source. Only once have I encountered a ghost who seemed to have gone dormant. When a family began renovating an old farmhouse, the former owner came out with a fury. While the energy generated by the workers tearing out the cabinets may have initially revived her—certainly enough to mess up almost every project they began and to set the contractor months behind schedule—she wasted no time in causing huge arguments between the husband and wife who owned the home. Because of the extensive work needed, they were not living in the farmhouse during renovation. Every time they visited the work site to see how things were progressing, they had a huge blowup. Even if they had agreed while driving over that they were going to most certainly, definitely, absolutely tell the contractor to go with the slate floor, after they'd been in the house for only a few minutes, they found themselves arguing over whether the floors should instead be refinished wood.

They finally called me, and I went out to talk to the ghost. She told me that for nearly fifty years, she'd just been very quietly sitting in the house. She was a tiny little thing—probably didn't weigh more than eighty pounds soaking wet. She'd gotten enough energy over the years from the occasional visitors to the house to survive. But when the work began, and she had enough energy to complain, boy did she make her presence known!

Ghosts Do Not Have Superpowers

The simple fact is that ghosts are just regular folks—who happen to be dead. I have noticed certain times when earthbound spirits seem to have more energy and be capable of moving physical objects, say, or creating the sensations of a physical presence to get your attention. When the moon is full or in the phase approaching full, most earthbound spirits seem to have access to energy that allows them to be more visibly active. Ghosts also need to be able to draw an amount of energy that corresponds to their size and personality when they were alive. For example, the little old lady ghost in the farmhouse certainly would not have the same energy needs as the earthbound spirit of a six-foot-four 185-pound stockbroker who ran marathons for fun!

I guess the only thing that earthbound spirits can do that might be considered supernatural is travel from place to place without transportation. Earthbound spirits have described their mode of travel to me as "I just think about going [from point A to point B] and then I'm there." Still, I have encountered plenty of earthbound spirits who prefer to travel by train, bus, or plane. These ghosts are not hitching a ride, however. They are usually attached to one of the living travelers. As a bonus, from the spirit's point of view, public transportation provides a great source of energy. Think of all the nervous fliers, harried travelers, and beleaguered families found on any single airline flight.

Ghosts Do Not Announce Their Presence with Cold Spots

One of the most common misconceptions about ghosts is that they cause a cold spot whenever they come into a room. People love to talk about these cold spots. I've always thought it sprang from the old wives' tale that thinking about a ghost will make you feel cold. Folks have often told me, "Well, it's cold in this corner all the time, so I know that's where the ghost stands." The truth is that, while earthbound spirits can create slight temperature changes, they're subtle—much like a slightly warm or cool breeze that flows past you briefly. If you have animals in your house, you may notice that they seem to be attuned to temperature changes you can't detect. Dogs may shiver suddenly on a warm day or begin panting when the house is cool.

Ghosts Can't Walk Through You—and You Cannot Walk Through Them

Animals are also better than humans at being able to detect the presence of an earthbound spirit in a room. One lady called me because her dog had developed a very strange pattern of behavior. The ground floor of their house was connected through doorways, making sort of a circular track. A couple of times a day, the energetic young dog would race in circles through the house, just doing laps until his energy was spent and he'd collapse on the floor. The family was used to this behavior and even thought their pet was pretty smart to have found a way to burn off his excess energy.

Suddenly though, the dog's behavior totally changed. He'd jump up and begin to race through the house, as always, but when he passed through the living room he'd do whatever he could to avoid a certain spot in the center: dodge or twist or come skidding to a halt. The woman told me that it looked as if the dog was trying to avoid knocking down a person standing in front of him.

Sure enough, when I arrived at the house, I came upon the ghost of an old man who liked to stand in the center of the living room, in front of the bay windows, and gaze across the property. He was a stubborn old guy, and he was not going to let some overenthusiastic puppy move him from his preferred viewing position. By the same token, the dog was determined to get around the ghost.

Most ghosts will move out of your way if you are headed toward them. More than once, I have seen a startled ghost leap out of the comfortable chair he or she was sitting in to avoid being crushed by a homeowner who, shaken by some piece of news I had given them, abruptly felt the need to sit down.

Earthbound spirits do not walk through walls. They prefer to use doors, just as they did when they were living. I guess ingrained habits are hard to break. Now, the doors don't have to be open, but ghosts definitely prefer to pass through an actual doorway. One exception to this rule is ghosts who hang out at colleges; they don't seem to care whether they use a door or scramble in through a second-floor window, especially if there's a fire escape nearby. When I am clearing college dorm rooms, I always place protective quince seeds—which prevent ghosts from reentering a home—over both the doorway *and* the windows.

Ghosts Can Interact with the Living to Create Danger and Cause Physical Harm

Ghosts draw energy from the new and full moons. In the days just preceding these lunar events, you may be able to feel an earthbound spirit's increased power. A ghost may come up behind you and blow on the back of your neck; one might pull at your hair, shake your mattress, or pull off your covers while you're asleep at night. You may notice doors opening or closing on their own, items falling off shelves, or wire hangers rattling in closets; you could find yourself more frequently "misplacing" household items such as keys, checkbooks, or important papers.

And while some ghosts may be more adept than others at interacting with the physical world around them, the idea—perpetuated by horror movies—that a ghost could kill a person or directly endanger a life through a physical altercation is basically untrue. Despite varying degrees of ability to interact with the physical world, ghosts will not stab, choke, or punch you, or push you down a flight of steps. Although I have infrequently seen physical evidence of an earthbound spirit interacting with a living person, I have yet to see a ghost kill anyone. What I *have* come across are malicious spirits who may indirectly influence the environment, resulting in harm to the living around them.

I once watched a ghost at our local YMCA purposely contribute to the near drowning of a woman. When I got into the pool for my water aerobics class, I wasn't surprised to see the ghost of a young man hanging around on the bleachers. Ghosts are pretty common at gyms; most are attached to someone who is working out, but there are always some who've wandered in just to take advantage of the energy generated when groups of people gather.

This young guy didn't look like he'd be attached to any of the other middle-aged women in my class, and normally I would have dismissed him and concentrated on the exercises. But something about this guy unnerved me, and so I kept an eye on him as I began my routine.

At first he just prowled the edges of the pool, sitting in the bleachers for a moment, strolling from the shallow end to the deep. He even climbed up into the lifeguard's chair and stood there, surveying the whole pool. There was another aerobics class being held in the deep end, and I watched, amazed, as the ghost got out of the chair, went to the edge of the pool, and slipped into the water along with the class. I had never seen a ghost choose to go swimming before, and when he ducked underwater, I scanned that end of the pool, waiting to see where he would surface.

I was still looking for him when there was a huge commotion. One of the women in the deep-water aerobics class suddenly dipped underwater. She resurfaced momentarily, thrashing her arms and screaming. From the way she was flailing around, it was clear that she was somehow in trouble.

The lifeguard and the aerobics instructor immediately jumped into the pool and towed her to the edge. It was then that I noticed a foam flotation device drifting slowly away from the other exercisers in her group.

I looked around the pool area again, but I couldn't see the ghost anywhere. I had a strong feeling that he'd had something to do with the woman's flotation device coming off. After my class ended, I ran into the woman in the locker room and had the chance to ask her if she was okay. She was clearly still shaken, and admitted to me that she probably shouldn't have been in the deep water at all, but she had just purchased a new type of flotation device and had felt confident that she'd be secure.

She showed me the float device—a foam belt clipped into

place with plastic clasps, like those used in a baby's high chair. She put the belt back on as she explained how it worked, and, judging by her difficulty in fastening the clasps, there was no way it could have come undone on its own.

She was clearly embarrassed by the whole affair, and I didn't want to make the situation any more uncomfortable by asking her if she knew some dead twenty-year-old who had it in for her. Maybe if she had said something like *You know, this kind of thing keeps happening ever since my stepson died*, I would have felt more comfortable offering to help. But I just couldn't bring myself to intrude.

While it seems clear that this ghost was intent on causing trouble and perhaps even putting this woman in real danger, he didn't directly try to drown her. I didn't see him try to pull her under or stand on her shoulders to push her down, even when she was thrashing around in the water. In fact, he seemed to vanish after undoing the belt. To me, this is reassuring evidence that although a ghost can conspire to put you in harm's way—by tampering with your electricity or wiring, which could cause a fire; or by loosening a board on the stairs, which could cause a fall—earthbound spirits cannot on their own directly cause the death of a living person.

Ghosts Do Not Always Announce Their Presences with Scents, Sounds, or Slime

In the movie *Ghostbusters*, the ghosts announce themselves with blasts of ectoplasmic slime. In real life, I can't say that I have ever identified the presence of an earthbound spirit by detecting slime or any other kind of sticky, oozing substance.

By the same token, I've never encountered ghosts who announced their presence by rattling chains and saying *Boo*. I have, however, seen some earthbound spirits deliver a resounding kick to a home's furnace, resulting in a serious *boom* that could scare you right out of your bed!

Interestingly enough, in the European castles I've been invited to visit, the ghosts *do* moan—a sort of *woe is me* wailing—as they roam the same hallways and stairwells over and over again. These are ghosts who look as if they died in the fourteenth, fifteenth, or sixteenth century. When the castles are open to tourists, the furnishings and rooms have usually been kept as true as possible to their original state. It seems to me that the spirits who roam these rooms feel it's their duty to continue patrolling the family estates. Although I've been invited to visit many castles, no owner has ever asked me to clear one of its spirits. To the owners, these "family ghosts" are invaluable tourist attractions. You wouldn't believe how many people are willing to pay to spend the night in an authentic haunted castle.

I have also heard people talk about ghosts appearing as a dense and shifting fog. People have described these "density spirits" to me as a being on different energy vibrations, which can be sorted by colors corresponding to a spirit's level of being. (For instance, I have heard people who claim to see black, dense shadows that are from hell but are moving around on the earthly plane.) I can't say definitely whether these kinds of apparitions exist, but they're not the types of ghosts that I can see. In fact, I've never seen a ghost who didn't look human.

Some, but not most, earthbound spirits do have a definite scent associated with them. For instance, those who died in a fire usually smell of smoke. On a few occasions, homeowners who persistently smell a burning or smoky odor in their home have called me for help, and it has turned out that they are sharing their home with a ghost who perished in a fire. A few people have reported smelling tobacco or cigarettes, and in some of those cases it turned out that their ghost had enjoyed smoking a pipe or had a three-pack-a-day habit.

But I have also been in houses where, although the homeowner swore there was a distinctive odor, I couldn't sense any earthbound spirits. One woman called me after her grandmother had died. She explained that she had taken some of her grandmother's furniture. They had put Grandma's rocker in the family room, and even when it was empty, that chair rocked back and forth a mile a minute. The woman also mentioned that whenever she walked past the room when the chair was moving, she could smell her grandmother's signature perfume, a distinctive scent called Evening in Paris.

Given all the signs, I couldn't blame the woman for thinking that the ghost of her grandmother had moved in and reclaimed her rocking chair, but I did not pick up on any earthbound spirits in her home. I reassured the woman that I believed her grandmother had crossed over into the Light and was fine, although it was possible that she just stopped by to visit from time to time.

What Ghosts Know and Don't Know

Ghosts Know That They Are Dead

Sometimes people ask me if spirits become earthbound because they don't realize they're dead. Simple common sense tells me that spirits can look down at their bodies and know they are dead. Talking to countless spirits at funeral homes confirms this. Although the spirits of very young children are rarely present at wakes or viewings, I have talked to the spirits of kids as young as five or six who tell me, "Well, I know it looks like I'm sleeping, but really, I'm dead."

In fact, I have yet to meet any spirits who didn't know they were dead. They may not *like* being dead, but they're aware that they are, and they know how they died. This is one of the reasons that I am able to help government and law enforcement agencies: Any homicide victims who have seen their murderers can identify them, especially if they knew their killers in life.

Earthbound Spirits Don't Have Any Special, Higher Knowledge

Until spirits cross into the Light, they do not gain any knowledge of what happens beyond the lives of mortals. Earthbound spirits cannot tell the future. They cannot predict the winning numbers in the lottery. They cannot offer special guidance or protection, or relay messages or information from spirits who have crossed over and are of the Light. There are spirits that some people refer to as "lying spirits." These ghosts will go out of their way to give wrong information to a medium or communicate the wrong answers on a Ouija board. Honestly, I don't consider this to be a special category of spirit. If your uncle Louie was a big liar when he was alive, he'll still be a big ol' liar when he is dead! If Aunt Elsie didn't have the answers to certain questions in life, she won't be any smarter as an earthbound spirit.

Some mediums claim to get information from angels or spirit guides. When these people have consistently correct information, I have to assume it's coming from an entity who's not earthbound. I have stood next to some of the most respected and consistently correct psychics in the country and seen no earthbound spirits next to them when they did their readings. I have to think that their information is coming from a spirit who has gone into the Light.

Ghosts do, however, have access to some kinds of information that they might not have been able to gain while they were alive, simply because they can move about and observe people undetected. Still, the fact that your kindly old neighbor who passed away can stop by to peek in on your morning beauty rituals does not count as her having higher knowledge, at least not in my book!

This kind of gossipy information that earthbound spirits are privy to can make my job difficult at times. I once was called to a house where a sexy-looking ghost named Dixie was wreaking havoc in a couple's relationship. I'd heard enough by the time Dixie had explained that she had followed the husband, Frank, home from a topless bar and that his wife, Candy, was a real piece of work. Did I really want to know that Frank had given Candy a diamond bracelet that she had secretly returned because she didn't think it had enough stones? And was it really necessary for the ghost to tell me that Candy had gone on a lingerie-shopping spree . . . but Frank wasn't the one who was going to be surprised by the lacy treats? No, this was definitely a case of my hearing more than I ever cared to know. Unfortunately, this kind of petty gossiping goes on fairly frequently. When I realize there's a threat of becoming caught up in such a soap opera, I do everything I can to encourage the homeowner to allow me to release the ghost into the Light as quickly as possible, with a minimum of questioning.

Detecting Earthbound Spirits

Many people claim to have various ways of detecting earthbound spirits. For me, it's easy. I simply see them standing in front of me. And, as I have explained, I can also see them in a specific building if I'm talking to someone in that building by phone. My daughter Tara, who can see and communicate with earthbound spirits just as I can, gets a tremendous headache in their presence, which disappears once she releases them.

I have heard of people who use energy meters and other devices to detect spirits. I don't understand how they work, or what kind of energy they are meant to detect, but the only experience I have ever had with seeing one operate was inconclusive at best.

I had done a lot of work for a very nice family in the Cleveland area. They first invited me to deal with some ghosts who had bad attitudes and a tendency to bother the family pets. Rick was self-employed as a general contractor, and some of the ghosts had followed him home from various work sites. I cleared their house for them, and we stayed in touch occasionally.

With the real estate market booming, Rick started a new business flipping homes. He'd go into a fringe neighborhood, scoop up a run-down house, renovate it, and sell it for a good profit. Often these houses came with a fairly bad history—they'd been drug dens, for instance, or scenes of violent crimes. Over time, Rick noticed that some were more problematic to work on than others. When he ran into a particularly challenging rehab project, he'd call me in; I'd go clear out whatever unsavory ghosts were hanging around and making the work more challenging.

Now, Rick was a real do-it-yourselfer type of guy. It was his philosophy that he should never pay someone to do anything he could do for himself. And so I wasn't entirely surprised when he called me one day from a new project and asked if any ghosts were on the site. There were. He told me to skip the details and just come on out.

When I arrived, I let myself in the front door and called out to Rick that I was there. He was working upstairs and said he'd be right down. While I waited for him, I noticed a strange machine that looked sort of like a canister vacuum sitting in the center of one of the rooms. I also noticed three earthbound spirits hanging around in various corners.

Rick came down and went right to the machine. "Check this out," he said. "I've gotten really good at this."

I had no idea what he was talking about, so I just nodded.

"Tell me how many ghosts are here," he said. "But don't give me any other information."

I told him there were three ghosts in the house.

"Okay," he said, pressing a button on the machine. "This time I'm going to tell *you* where they are."

He began to walk around the room, waving the tube attached to the end of the machine around like a wand. The machine made a low humming noise and sometimes emitted a series of clicks, sort of like a Geiger counter.

I leaned against the door frame, just watching. I'm always open to learning something new. Rick circled the room a couple of times before coming to a stop in front of the fireplace. His machine was clicking like crazy.

"There's one right here," he said confidently.

"I don't see anything," I said.

Rick's face fell. "There's nothing there?" He moved to another part of the room. "How about here?"

I told him there was a ghost standing on the first landing of the stairs, and he moved toward that area, but the machine stayed silent.

"Stupid thing," Rick said, roughly switching the machine off. "I think I've been ripped off for 450 bucks."

I didn't totally disbelieve that the machine was reading something. "Maybe it does pick up other kinds of entities," I suggested. I reminded him that I couldn't see anything other than earthbound spirits, but that didn't mean that other kinds of beings weren't in the room.

But Rick remained disappointed.

Having had time to think about it, I now wonder if Rick's machine wasn't similar to those I've seen ghost hunters use on television shows. Perhaps these devices are accurate at reading certain kinds of energies. What I do know is that the one time I saw one live in action, it certainly didn't pick up on any of the same ghosts I was seeing.

Summoning Earthbound Spirits

Inviting a ghost into your home is *never* a good idea. Nevertheless, I can't tell you how many people have called me after experimenting with Ouija boards, automatic writing, black magic, or other dark practices. There are even people who go to funerals or cemeteries and issue open invitations to ghosts to come home with them; they think it would be "cool" to have a haunted house. I can't stress enough what a plain old *bad* idea this is. The presence of an earthbound spirit can cause a host of problems, from physical ailments such as an increase in colds or upper respiratory problems, to mechanical problems like malfunctioning furnaces or electrical issues, to minor inconveniences such as constantly misplaced keys or lost checkbooks.

Using a Ouija board and attending a séance are two of the most popular methods curious people use to try to communicate with their loved ones. Often the spirits people are seeking to communicate with have already crossed over; instead of talking to dear old Grandma, those present can be tricked by earthbound spirits who tell them things designed to provoke strong reactions and create the kind of emotional energy that ghosts need to survive.

Where Ghost Congregate

Contrary to popular belief, cemeteries are not the most haunted spots on earth. Other than ghosts who attend their graveside services, it is uncommon to find an earthbound spirit hanging around a graveyard. A ghost—most often an older person—may stop by the cemetery on occasion to see if his or her grave site is being properly tended to by the family. But earthbound spirits need energy, and there's not a lot of it available from the occasional groundskeeper, custodian, or family visiting a loved one's grave.

I was once asked to be the featured speaker for a local cemetery association meeting. I'm asked to do this sort of thing fairly often, and since this was a local organization, I figured the members had probably heard me on the radio or read articles about my work in the local press. I expected that I'd be able to talk to several interesting spirits at whatever restaurant or banquet hall they had chosen for their meeting. Restaurants are great places to find ghosts, either attached to the property or coming and going with diners.

Imagine my surprise when it was announced that the venue for my speech would be a newly built mausoleum. I admit I was a bit worried that I would have to stand up in front of a gathering of funeral directors and cemetery caretakers and tell them that there were no spirits present, because they rarely spent time in cemeteries.

Luckily for me, three ghosts had decided to attend the meeting as well. They had come in with some of the guests—which is a bit unusual, since, despite their line of work, funeral directors do not usually tend to attract earthbound spirits. One of the ghosts was actually attached to the caretaker at a nearby cemetery.

The funeral directors who worked most closely with that facility were also the most skeptical of the group. They kept exchanging glances that made it clear they had their doubts about what I was saying.

The ghost told me that the caretaker had been having a lot of trouble with equipment lately, specifically the lawn mowers. When I mentioned this, the two directors looked at each other.

"Has Charlie over at the grounds mentioned any trouble with the lawn mowers?" the man coolly asked his colleague.

"Perhaps he said something . . . ," the woman who was with him replied.

"If by *something* they mean that the lawn mower crashed through the office walls last week," the ghost muttered to me.

I related what he'd said. Apparently the story of the runaway lawn mower had been circulating among the different directors and cemeteries, because more than half the room burst out laughing. The two skeptics who had been such cool customers made sure that they'd be seated at my table when we later moved to a restaurant.

Before we could adjourn for dinner, however, I had one more order of business. One of the ghosts was a woman who was extremely unhappy with her burial plot. When the mausoleum we were standing in was built, resting places were created both on the inside and outside of the structure. Mrs. Tobin's earthbound spirit had been hanging around the cemetery, hoping to be able to get someone's attention. Her family, at the last moment, had ignored her wishes to be buried inside the mausoleum, choosing an outdoor spot for her final resting place.

I explained her concerns to the manager in charge of the mausoleum; he promised to contact the family and offer to move the body inside. When he did so later on, the family asked to meet with me first. After asking their mother's ghost several questions, they apologized for being cheap and requested that her body be moved. With a very satisfied expression, Mrs. Tobin's earthbound spirit was only too happy to cross over into the Light.

Although funeral directors and cemetery caretakers interact with the dead all the time, they do not tend to bring ghosts home from work. Most earthbound spirits go into the Light after the funeral. Those determined to stay usually follow a family member home. But certain types of businesses are definitely at high risk for attracting earthbound spirits. In the final part of this book, I'll talk more about this issue, but here is a partial list of some very common places for earthbound spirits to spend time: shopping malls, supermarkets, carnivals and amusement parks, concerts, hospital emergency rooms, bars—the seedier, the better—nursing homes, dentists' offices, theaters, airplanes, law offices, publishing offices, rehab facilities, and police stations.

Basically, ghosts will gather anywhere they are likely to find sources of physical and emotional energy. Think of a movie cineplex, for instance, with all the emotional energy generated by a crowd gasping at the latest thriller or horror film, or sobbing their way through a heartbreaking love story.

For most ghosts, drawing on this emotional energy is enough, although I'll never forget one who had apparently decided to up the ante by wreaking havoc in a movie house. Ted and I had gone out on a Friday-night date to see a popular film in a theater near our house. We loaded up on treats from the concession stand and found seats toward the back of the crowded theater.

As people began filing in to take their seats, I noticed a woman appear to stumble, her popcorn flying out of the tub and showering back down around her. As she turned and studied the floor, trying to figure out what she might have tripped over, I noticed that she paid no attention to the teenager standing in the aisle slightly behind her. The kid had a huge grin plastered across his face. As I watched, he stepped out in front of another woman who was also carrying a large tub of popcorn and quickly tapped on the bottom of the tub. The popcorn went flying as the startled moviegoer jumped back and lost her balance.

I have to admit that at first I was somewhat amused as I watched him pull this same prank on several more unsuspecting people. One woman even dragged the theater manager down the aisle, convinced that it was the sticky floor that had caused her to stumble. But then things got a little mean. The ghost targeted a family with a harassed-looking mother and father and three kids. The oldest child was holding a gigantic tub of popcorn, and the ghost gave it a real whack. The tub went flying and the father smacked the kid upside the head, ignoring the child's protests that he'd been careful. The teen kept up his routine until nearly everyone was seated and the previews had started. Frankly, I was getting sick of it. When an elderly man using a walker began to make his way down the aisle as his equally elderly wife followed with their small bags of popcorn and I saw the ghost start to move toward them, I had had enough. I looked right at him. "You just cut that out right now," I said clearly.

The ghost stared at me. It was clear by his expression that he knew he'd been busted. "That's right," I said. "I'm talking to you, and it's just not funny anymore."

It was obvious to me that the ghost's prank created enough stress in the audience to give him a large dose of energy. I didn't see if he stayed to watch the movie or not; most likely he just moved on, returning to wherever he spent most of his time, energized by his evening out at the movies.

Never Say Never

Perhaps the most important thing my experiences with earthbound spirits have taught me is that ghosts aren't really all that different from the living. With more than fifty years of communicating with earthbound spirits as reference, I have become pretty good a predicting certain behaviors from certain types of ghosts. But I know it would be a mistake to become complacent. While I can go for years without encountering a particular type of earthbound spirit—one who is truly dark or malevolent, for instance (more on them in chapter 9), or an incubus or succubus who can sexually interact with the living—I do know that they're out there.

Through the course of my work, I have gone all over the world and met all kinds of people—and I still haven't lost my ability to be amazed by personalities. So I'm not really surprised when I encounter earthbound spirits who behave unexpectedly. In fact, I'm usually grateful for the fresh insight into some aspect of an earthbound spirit's existence. And while all my years of experience have led me to believe that certain things about earthbound spirits are largely true while others are largely the product of misinformation or media portrayals, I'm also careful to recognize that each new meeting with a spirit brings the potential for me to gain fresh insight and information. I think this is why, after so many years, I still enjoy my work. And even though on a daily basis the information I learn and the ghosts I communicate with can be quite ordinary, I am confident that there are still surprises out there awaiting me.

3

THE WHITE LIGHT

An Opportunity to Cross Over

I USE THE white Light for a very specific purpose in my work as a paranormal investigator. And although I discovered how I could use the Light decades ago, other people were doing so for many years before me. During the seventeenth century, Sir Isaac Newton proved that white light is the effect of combining, in equal proportions, all the visible colors of light. The result is a pure color that is rich in symbolism. In many cultures, the color white is associated with purity, clarity, and good. People who work in the metaphysical or spiritual arts often describe or use white light in the context of their healing work. White light may be used in yoga or meditation practices. Other people talk about its protective powers.

When I was a young girl, the nuns at my Catholic school would tell Bible stories that often featured blinding bursts of light: angels arriving in dramatic flashes; Moses encountering a bush that was consumed by pure flame but not burned. Today I think of white Light as a manifestation of positive energy, and later in this book I will tell you how you can begin to access the special powers of this potent force.

The White Light and Earthbound Spirits

In my everyday work with earthbound spirits, however, the white Light plays a very particular and critical role. Over many years of observing this Light, I have come to several conclusions. Others who work with the Light may have different interpretations or uses for it, and I'll be the first to admit that I don't know everything there is to know. I honestly don't expect that I'll understand everything about this powerful force until I die and have a chance to walk into it myself. What I do know about the Light, I've learned from both personal experience and from talking to spirits who have had the chance to go into it but refused—for any number of reasons.

The white Light that comes to people when they die serves a very practical purpose. If you listen to folks recount near-death experiences, they are likely to talk about how they could see friends and loved ones in a blindingly bright light, as if at the end of a long tunnel, and how these familiar figures were gesturing as if to welcome the dead person into their company. Usually people will admit that they felt a strong impulse to move toward this Light, to join their friends and family in what seemed to be a welcoming and peaceful place. They repeat that they felt good; though they were aware they weren't with their bodies, they were not uncomfortable. But sometimes these people suddenly experience a compelling urge to return to their bodies—and when they do, the Light disappears. In a medical setting, this is referred to as a near-death experience. Doctors who have performed heroic measures on someone officially declared dead will credit the person's return to life to medical science. I credit free will.

But when you do take your last breath for real, that bright white Light will be there for you. If death is imminent, the Light may come earlier. For instance, I have seen people on life support who have the Light with them. And although I can't see it, I believe that those who are lingering with a terminal illness may have the Light around them for some time—perhaps as long as a week prior to their death. I think it's a way to ease their fears—to let them know there is something more waiting for them when their body ceases to function. Hospice nurses will talk of sitting with patients near death who will moan and groan and speak to an unseen presence in the corner of the room. When asked whom they're speaking to, they'll respond with something like "It's Ralph, my brother, and he's standing right there." The comforting presence seems palpable, even to the nurse and the family who are aware that Ralph has been dead for years.

Every time I have asked spirits if they can see anyone in the white Light, they tell me they can. If I ask them who it is they're seeing, they name names. But when I look at that very same Light, I do not see any figures within it. It just looks like a bright white light to me. Interestingly, people who are near death—but still alive—when the white Light comes to them can communicate with the people they see within the Light. But once they're dead and their spirits have left their bodies, they can no longer talk to—or hear—the spirits who have crossed over. At funerals, ghosts will frequently ask me about this. "Why won't they talk to me?" they'll ask, gesturing toward the Light. "I was talking to them yesterday, and now they won't say anything. Are they mad at me?"

I explain to these spirits that now that they, too, are dead, they need to go into the Light to communicate with those people they see in it. After considering this phenomenon for a number of years, I have decided that for those who are nearing death, the familiar faces and voices from within the Light may provide comfort at an uncertain, perhaps even frightening, time. After death, when people's spirits are released from their bodies, it is a matter of free will to step into the Light and cross over.

I cannot communicate with those spirits who have crossed over or gone into this Light, although I do have friends who are mediums who are able to. And I do know that spirits who have crossed over have the ability to appear in dreams, while for earthbound spirits this is extremely difficult and rare. I also know, from talking to earthbound spirits who can see their loved ones gesturing to them from within the Light, that when spirits pass into the Light, they become visible as their best selves. What I mean by this is that, if folks were ill or elderly or disfigured when they died, within the Light they regain their appearance from their most vital years. One of the most touching examples of this phenomenon came during an encounter with the ghost of a lovely, elderly lady who had been earthbound for many years.

As I do in all houses that I am clearing of ghosts, I allowed the homeowner to ask questions of the spirit in her house. We learned that the woman was ninety-three when she died and that she had lived a long and happy life with her husband, who had died ten years before her. During the conversation, it became clear to me that she still missed her dear companion. I was certain that when I made the white Light, she would eagerly embrace the opportunity to be united with her true love.

To my surprise, when I asked her if she was ready to go into the Light, she adamantly refused. "I didn't go the first time and I won't go now" was all she would say, no matter how much I cajoled her.

"Don't you want to be with your husband?" I asked.

It broke my heart to see the tears running down her cheeks. "I saw him in the Light the first time," she said. "He looked so young and handsome."

Holding her thin arms out in front of her and gazing at her shaking hands, she continued, "I'm an old lady. Look at me: I'm wrinkled and gray, and I can't even stand up straight. What would my handsome husband want now with an old dame like me?"

When I understood her fears, I was able to reassure her that she, like her husband, would return to her prime. "You'll join your husband and you'll be a really cute couple again," I promised her as I made the Light.

And as she straightened up as much as she could and walked into the brightness, I truly believed that she was heading into the same kind of love and happiness she had known as a newlywed.

The White Light and When to Cross Over

Of course, there are some spirits who are ready to leave the earth as soon as they have departed from their bodies. But even for those willing to go, there is no great rush. In fact, as you'll read in chapter 5 about funerals, almost all ghosts stay to attend their own.

When I was younger and regularly attending funerals with my grandmother, I sometimes wondered what spirits did from the time I saw them at their viewings until their memorial services were finished and they stepped into the white Light that hovered near them at their grave in the cemetery. Perhaps they had unfinished business and traveled from person to person or place to place to see for themselves that all loose ends were tied up to their satisfaction.

But I also learned that for some ghosts waiting to go into the Light, it was just a matter of timing. After a few years of marriage, Ted and I moved with our two young daughters into a small house on a private street. Just outside and across the street from the house was St. Bridget's Cemetery. At the bottom of the hill, on the county road running past our home, was another large cemetery. Living so close to two graveyards didn't bother me at all when we bought the house. Ghosts do not hang out in cemeteries. The energy from other living creatures is vital to their continued strength: They seek out people and crowds. Frankly, for ghosts, cemeteries are just too quiet.

One day I came up from our basement and was shocked to see three ghosts sitting at my dining room table. Now, I had never before (and only once since) had any ghosts in any of my other houses. Naturally I was curious. "Hey, who are you, and what are you doing here?" I asked.

Normally, ghosts are shocked that I can see them, but these three didn't bat an eye. They glanced up at me, but none of them said a word. I could see that they all had their white Light around them, so obviously they had not been dead for long.

I went into the kitchen to start dinner, wondering whether anyone we knew from town might have passed away and needed to talk to me. But we were fairly new to the area, and I couldn't think of a single person. About half an hour later and still puzzling over my strange visitors, I went back into the dining room to set the table—and the three were gone.

That night, after dinner and putting the kids to bed, Ted and I were sitting in the living room. It was just a normal night at home: me reading the local paper, Ted snoozing in his armchair. The phone rang, and when I got up to answer it, I passed through the dining room. My three ghostly visitors were back. This time they didn't even acknowledge me with a look. They just sat at the table, staring into space.

I had absentmindedly carried the paper into the kitchen with me when I went to answer the phone, and after the call, I opened it to the obituaries. Like most small local papers, ours included photographs of the deceased along with the death notices. I checked the photos, then peeked out into the dining room, and then double-checked the paper. Sure enough, two of the ghosts sitting in my dining room had their photos in that evening's edition. I read their death notices. The viewings at the funeral home were being held from six to nine o'clock that very night. I wondered why the ghosts weren't there. From their obituaries, I knew they had died in nursing homes. Perhaps they didn't have much family, or didn't expect anyone to be at the viewing. Even more poignantly, maybe they had gone to the funeral home only to find that no one had come to say a final good-bye before the burial services at the local cemeteries.

The three ghosts were still sitting at the table when Ted and I went to bed that night. And the next morning, all three were gone. For the rest of the time that we lived in this house, I would occasionally come across different ghosts hanging out in my dining room, as if it were a waiting room where they could pass the time between their viewing at the funeral home and their burial service at the cemetery.

Of course, this is only speculation. To my great frustration, I could never get any of the spirits who passed their final time on earth sitting at my dining room table to talk to me. Not once.

Nevertheless, from other experiences—and after attending innumerable funerals—I've concluded that the white Light stays with people for about seventy-two to eighty hours after their last memorial service. For instance, if someone dies away from home, and there is a burial there and then a second service at home, it could be a week or ten days until that final service. After the last service, the Light will remain for the seventy-two- to eighty-hour window, gradually growing dimmer and smaller, until spirits can no longer walk into it and cross over.

The Light is with spirits from the moment they leave their bodies until the end of this "grace period." During this time, I can see or talk to any spirit who has not gone into the Light, but spirits are not considered "officially" earthbound until their Light has disappeared. I can see these spirits as clearly as I see any other living person. And I can talk to them and hear their answers. I don't often speak aloud—our conversations appear silent to anyone watching—which is partly why what I do can seem so darned *uninteresting* to anyone expecting a big supernatural show. Although ghosts can't read the thoughts of the living, they can hear everything that is said aloud. Think about *that* the next time you're at the funeral of that mean old aunt you always resented and have the urge to share a piece of juicy gossip about her with other family members!

In fact, the best advice I can give about attending a funeral is: If you can't say anything nice, it's better not to say anything at all. Because I guarantee you that the ghost of the person who has died is standing right there in the room with you, taking in every word. At just about every funeral I've attended—and I've been at some doozies—the spirit of the deceased stands at the foot of the coffin surveying the crowd, checking out the flowers, and eavesdropping on the subdued murmurs of the mourners.

Why Spirits Stay

Over the years, I've heard as many reasons for staying earthbound as there are individuals, but generally I have found that whatever people were like when they were alive, so they are when they're dead—maybe even more so. Responsible people stay because they think they can help; control freaks stay because they want everything to be just so, even after they're gone; folks with big egos stay because they assume others will miss them too much; people with guilty consciences stay because they are afraid of judgment or punishment; social butterflies stay because they love being the guest of honor at their own funerals, and by the time they realize that all the services are over and everyone who gathered to talk about them has begun to return to daily life, their Light has faded and gone and they're stuck. Snoops, spies, and generally nosy people stick around for the thrill of unlimited access—they can go anywhere, hear and see anything—it's irresistible. The truth is that there is no good reason to remain earthbound. And part of my job is to explain this to the spirits I encounter.

I remember one little girl spirit whom I met when a mother asked me to come and clear their house of a ghost intimidating her four-year-old daughter. I learned that Lana, a formerly friendly and outgoing child, had become increasingly withdrawn and secretive, spending hours in her playroom with her "best friend," Suzy.

At first Lana's mother, Donna, had assumed that Suzy was an imaginary friend, a figment of her young daughter's lively imagination. But the more Lana told her mother about Suzy— how she had followed Lana and her babysitter home from the playground; how she told Lana not to let her mother or grandparents into the playroom; and finally, and most disturbingly, how she'd told Lana that if anyone ever found out about her, she would burn the house down—the more worried Donna became.

When Lana began to come down with cold after cold, each more severe than the last, and continued to grow more withdrawn and anxious—all symptoms of sharing a home with an earthbound spirit—her mother knew she had to take action. That was when she called me.

When I arrived at their house, I immediately saw Suzy sulking on the stairs. "She's here," I confirmed for the worried parents.

Suzy looked to be about seven or eight. She had dark hair that fell in ringlets around her chubby face. Her fists were clenched against her sides, and she glared at me from under thick eyebrows. I could tell from her attitude that she was a bit of a bully. But I've raised two children and been a foster parent to many others, and I understand kids almost as well as I understand ghosts.

It didn't take me long to find out that Suzy had died in a house fire in the late 1940s. I wondered why she hadn't gone into the Light.

"Did your parents die in the fire, too?" I asked.

Suzy nodded.

"And did they go into the white Light? Could you see them?"

Suzy nodded again.

"Could you see anyone else?" I prodded.

"My grandma," she finally said.

"Wouldn't you like to see your mother and father again?" I asked gently.

To my surprise, Suzy frowned, stuck out her lower lip, and vigorously shook her head no.

I have learned that when children don't want to go into the Light, I must tread carefully. They may have seen an adult there of whom they are frightened—an alcoholic mother, an abusive father, a nasty grandparent. Fear can keep them from crossing over.

"What about your grandma?" I asked.

Suzy's face softened. "I do want to see Grandma," she whispered.

"But not Mom and Dad?" I persisted.

Suzy was silent for a few minutes. I waited. Finally she spoke.

"They're mad at me," she said in a small voice. "If I go to them, I'm going to be in trouble."

I suddenly felt sorry for her. "Why do you think you'll be in trouble?"

Suzy began to cry as she explained how she knew her parents had been in the house and died in the fire and how she knew she was supposed to go into the Light, but instead she had run away from the house. She'd tried to go back and find her parents, but—like any lost little kid—she'd become confused and disoriented and, before she knew it, her Light was gone.

"Oh, sweetie, they must miss you," I said. "They'll forgive you. I know, because I'm a mom."

"But I've been bad while I'm here. I've been mean to lots of kids, not just Lana," Suzy said, hanging her head.

I was not surprised to find out that ever since she had become earthbound, Suzy had wandered from house to house, seeking the familiar environment of a family and the company of children her age. When people die, their spirits remain at the age they were at their death. Child ghosts seek out children, but when the living children grow up, the ghosts move on, searching for the next place where they feel they can fit in.

It seems to be a particularly difficult existence for child spirits, and I always do everything I can to encourage them to cross over. They almost always do. Suzy was no exception. I reassured her again that her parents would forgive her and made the white Light for her to enter. "It's okay to go," I said gently as she stepped toward the Light. "Your grandmother can help you explain things to your parents."

It's not only children who will hesitate to go into the Light. I have met many other spirits, especially those who have committed suicide, who are afraid that they will be judged or punished if they cross over.

Just like these spirits, I, too, wonder what awaits us in the Light. I have asked all kinds of spiritual leaders whether they can tell me if earthbound spirits are in purgatory or hell or some other kind of limbo, and what they believe happens once they cross into the Light. But no one has been able to give me a satisfactory answer. The one thing they all agree on, however, is that spirits are not meant to remain on earth.

Although I'm Catholic, I do believe in a form of reincarnation. I feel that as long as a ghost remains earthbound, the spirit cannot go forward spiritually or emotionally or gain the higher form of awareness that I am sure is awaiting each of us in the Light. Basically, spirits who don't cross over become "stuck" here on earth. They cannot help the living in any way, and they do not know anything more about the workings of the afterlife than they did when they were alive.

What Awaits Us in the Light

When I run into spirits who have lost their white Light, I never hesitate to make it for them. I figure that everyone has the Light with them when they die, and everyone has the choice to cross over. So who am I to decide whether or not they should have a second chance? I believe my job is to make the Light, let the person walk into it, and let a higher power make the judgment about what happens after that. Once I have watched earthbound spirits go into the Light, I close it behind them. If they're going to heaven or to some other good place, then they'll be fine. If they're going to hell, I'm sure not going to be the one who leaves the door open for them to come back out. As far as I'm concerned, the road through the white Light only goes one way! Because I have never yet seen a spirit turn around and try to come back out of the Light, I suspect that not even ghosts know exactly where they are headed when they start on their journey into the Light. No matter how much reason they might have to fear judgment, or how much work I have to do to convince them to cross over, once ghosts agree to go into the Light, they all go willingly.

For instance, in one chilling encounter, I released the very disturbing spirit of a confirmed killer into the Light. I had gone to visit an elegant home in a wealthy community not far from Chicago after receiving a call from a woman—an antiques dealer—who thought that she might have ghosts in her house. It was likely that she did; ghosts often attach themselves to significant pieces of furniture or antique jewelry or collectibles. When I arrived at her elegant Victorian home, I wasn't surprised to find six ghosts, men and women of various ages, all of whom had entered the house along with different antique pieces the homeowner had collected. None of them knew the woman, and all of them willingly went into the Light.

It was after the six left that I turned my attention to another ghost who'd been lurking in a corner of the dining room and staring at me with what I can describe only as creepy eyes. I have to confess that he made me feel very uncomfortable. Even the homeowner picked up on the strange tension in the room.

"There's still someone here, isn't there?" she asked.

I glanced again at the man in the corner. He was tall and very thin, with dark, unkempt hair that fell in long, jagged bangs across his forehead. He was dressed in a weird, ill-fitting outfit that looked like a cross between a uniform and pajamas. But it wasn't his clothing that made me uneasy. It was the unblinking stare that he had fixed on me. His eyes were a strangely pale shade of blue and completely devoid of any emotion or warmth.

"There is someone here," I replied. "And he's just, well, not right."

"Who is he?" the woman asked nervously.

The ghost blinked for maybe the first time. A smile flitted across his face, but it didn't make him look any friendlier.

"She knows who I am," he said. "Everyone knows Harold Blakely."

Now, I certainly didn't know any Harold Blakely, but I wasn't going to mess with this guy's delusions of grandeur, either, so I just nodded.

"Tell *her*," he insisted, gesturing at the woman sitting across from me. "Tell her that I'm here."

Unnerved by my silence, the woman gestured toward me. "What's he saying?"

"I think maybe he's mentally unstable," I said to her. "He says that you know who he is, though."

I told her his name. She gasped.

"Oh, geez . . . so you do know him?" Now it was my turn to be amazed.

The woman nodded. She explained that her mother and Harold's mother had known each other long ago, when her family lived in Kentucky. The two had stayed in touch over the years and through several moves by each family. When the woman was a young college graduate, first living in Chicago, her mother and Harold's mother hatched up a plan for her to go on a date with Harold.

I looked from the elegant, successful woman sitting across from me to the creepy character standing in the corner and raised my eyebrow.

The woman nodded her understanding of my reaction. She had agreed to meet Harold once, she explained, but that one time was enough. She couldn't say exactly why, but he had simply freaked her out. She never went out with or spoke to him again.

"Trusting my instincts probably saved my life," she continued.

Clearly I was missing a piece of the whole picture. I must have looked as puzzled as I felt.

"Don't you remember the story from about fifteen years ago? The one about the guy in West Virginia who killed, chopped up, cooked, and ate his mother?"

I couldn't help it. I whipped my head around to stare at the ghost.

He just stared back with those creepy, expressionless eyes. "My mother was okay with it," he said calmly.

The woman told me what she knew of the rest of his story, Harold helpfully filling in the blanks. He had spent the rest of his life in a mental institution for the criminally insane, until just a few years ago when he had killed himself by suffocation. He'd been at this woman's house ever since.

"And she hasn't seen any other men since I've been here," he said with satisfaction.

I had no idea about what he was talking about, but when I relayed his comment to the woman, she laughed despite the circumstances.

"I think you've just solved the mystery of why I never get asked out on a second date," she said.

Usually I ask homeowners if they are ready to release the ghost. In this case, I already knew the answer. It was definitely time for Harold to move on. But I'll admit that I had a few questions: Would he see his mother in the Light? Would she be afraid? Angry? Forgiving? I didn't know. All I knew was that Harold couldn't stay here ruining this woman's life. And so I told him that his mother really wanted to see him. Then I made the Light and had him cross into it.

There are those who would criticize me for sending a remorseless murderer into the Light. My take on it is that this is my job. It's what I do. Who am I to decide or judge? There's no rulebook for sending earthbound spirits into the Light, and so I've had to make up my own rules as I've gone along. And one of my rules is that every spirit who has been earthbound should get a chance to leave.

For my own peace of mind, I have to believe that there is some power at the end of the Light deciding what becomes of spirits when they cross over. I have let murderers and criminals and liars and thieves into the same Light that I have made for sweet little grandmothers and angelic-looking children. It is impossible for me to believe that they are all going to the same place.

How and When I Make the White Light

Of course, I don't simply go around making the white Light randomly. What happens is that I get a call from someone having specific problems—health-related issues, problems with the mechanics of their home, or tension in a relationship that results in endless quarreling—and I can tell, from listening to their message or talking to them directly, if there is a ghost in their home or business. If so, I must go to where the ghost is to speak to him or her and to make the Light. Most people want the opportunity to talk to their ghosts. They want to confirm that it has, in fact, been the ghost who's been hiding the checkbook right around bill-paying time, or leaving the car keys in the most ridiculous places, or causing the furnace or the electrical systems or the car to malfunction almost constantly. Sometimes the person who calls knows the ghost. Most people don't.

After clients have exhausted their list of questions, I ask them if they are ready to release the ghost. Most people are only too glad to clear their home and have their lives return to normal. If they say yes, I make the white Light, just as my grandmother taught me to do when I was young, and tell the ghosts that they need to leave. I watch the ghosts walk away from me into the Light. It's as if I'm watching someone walk into a very bright tunnel. Some walk slowly, some quickly, some break into a run, a few turn to wave to me, and a few difficult cases have offered a less heartwarming "one-finger salute." When I cannot see their figures anymore, I close up the Light. Sometimes it's just that simple. Sometimes it's far more complicated.

When I first began doing this, as a child, I didn't have as sophisticated an understanding of what made spirits stay and what would convince them to leave as I do now. I'd simply make the Light, point to my grandmother, and tell the ghost, "My grandmother says you have to leave now." In those days, ghosts were as likely to tilt their heads and say something along the lines of "Awww, isn't she *cute*? She's telling her grandma what I said." These spirits were the ones who'd usually speak in the condescending baby-talk tone some adults seem to think children prefer to be addressed with. Others seemed puzzled. Obviously I could see them, but why should they take orders from a child? These ghosts might hesitate when

I first told them to leave, but after a glance at my grandmother, they'd turn and march right into that Light. Honestly, I can't remember any spirit ever refusing to go when I was a little girl!

When I was a teenager, I remember being annoyed if spirits gave me attitude. After all, I'd been doing this for years. And of course, anyone who has spent any time with teenagers will know what I mean when I say that I was always 100 percent convinced that I knew what was best for the spirit. As I matured and began to appreciate all the complex reasons spirits can have for remaining earthbound, I realized I had to learn how to manipulate stubborn ghosts into doing what I wanted them to do.

After years of practice in making the Light, I have learned how to control it very well. I can keep it open for longer periods of time to let in multiple ghosts. I can make it bigger or smaller. I've also gotten much better at convincing, coaxing, or ordering a reluctant ghost to cross over. Now that I'm older, I think the younger ghosts respect me as an authority figure and the older ghosts acknowledge me as a peer. Most are willing to go.

Sometimes earthbound spirits want to be sure I'll convey a message to a particular person. In most cases, I have no way of doing so—it's not like I'm going to call people out of the blue and tell them I have a message from a ghost! When I'm working with law enforcement, I do make sure I get the message to the proper authorities, but generally I feel it's most important to get spirits to cross over, so I tell them whatever I think will get them to go. Often the person they want to get a message to has been dead for many years. In these situations, I tell ghosts that the easiest way to convey the message is to go into the Light and deliver it themselves.

Once they have recovered from their shock that I can actually see and hear them, many earthbound spirits are grateful for the opportunity to cross over. They ask me to thank the person who called me in. Others look back gratefully, just before they step into the Light, as if to acknowledge and thank me.

When making the Light and watching spirits cross over, I'm always struck by the way ghosts retain the same personalities and social courtesies we expect of living people. In groups, it's generally "ladies before gentlemen"; adults will take children's hands to walk into the Light with them. I've had old racist ghosts refuse to go into the same Light as someone of a different color. And I've had law-abiding spirits refuse to share the Light with less morally upright folks. When these situations arise, I simply do the practical thing: I let one spirit into the Light, allow it to close, and then make it again.

It is not physically tiring or difficult for me to make the Light. When I'm trying to hold it open for several or many ghosts to cross over, however, I can become mentally fatigued. Several years ago, I was asked to come in and clear one of Cleveland's grand old theaters. Theaters are always full of ghosts. There are stagehands who can't bear to leave, actresses and actors reluctant to step out of the spotlight, aspiring stars who can't give up their dream of breaking out of the repertory company to headline a show, and the patrons themselves, who are thrilled to realize they have free unlimited access to every opening night. When I clear a theater, I go prepared to deal with a crowd.

At this particular theater, I spent most of the morning making the Light in three- or four-minute increments. And I have to admit, for the most part the spirits who were hanging around were very cooperative. The theater was well past its glory days and scheduled for renovation, and I guess most of the ghosts knew that they were overstaying their welcome. I would hold the Light open as men in top hats and women in sweeping gowns crossed over. Then I'd let it close, ask the others to wait a few minutes, and, after a brief rest, reopen it to the next group. By the end of the day I was exhausted, but the theater was empty.

When I clear a space of this size, I don't usually talk to the ghosts who are crossing over. I may notice some particularly striking people, just as anyone would when observing a large crowd. The funny thing about doing this theater was that, a few months later, I was asked to visit another of Cleveland's grand entertainment palaces. When I arrived, I actually recognized several of the ghosts from the first theater. Rather than crossing over, they had simply transferred their loyalties to another venue.

When Spirits Can't—or Won't—Cross Over

Of course, there are also times when either the homeowner or the ghost is less than cooperative. I've had people schedule appointments—but when I arrive at their houses and confirm the presence of a ghost, they tell me they want to "keep" their ghost. Frankly, I've never understood this. The reason people call me in the first place is that something is causing difficulties in their homes or lives. To decide that they want this energy to stay with them or insist that maybe a ghost can "help" or "guide" them is simply foolish.

Nevertheless, on the occasions when a homeowner refuses to let me release the spirit, I do not make the Light. Again, it's because I believe in free will—for both the living and the dead— even if folks want to continue to make their own lives difficult by allowing a spirit to remain attached to their property.

However, I will mention, out loud, that if ghosts in fact *wanted* to cross over, it was entirely possible for them to seek out a funeral home and simply use the Light of the recently deceased. At least this way, I figure the ghost is free to take my advice and find a way to cross over if that is what they wish.

On the other hand, there are the ghosts who are unwilling to leave. Most often these are folks who are nursing a grudge— sometimes decades old. These ghosts are fully aware of the discord they are causing, but are usually getting a sense of satisfaction from making the existence of the living as miserable as their own ghostly existence.

One family in particular suffered from the resentment that a dead brother held toward his living brother. The family had called me after years of incidents that centered on the boys of the family and their vehicles. The father who called had five sons. All of these boys had horrible luck with cars: electrical malfunctions, mechanical failures, a tendency toward fender benders. When the father called me, it was because four of the five boys had recently been in fairly serious auto accidents. Gradually, each admitted that right before each accident, he'd been distracted by a glimpse of a kid sitting in the previously empty backseat. What was even weirder, they all agreed, was that the kid looked just like their father had when he was young.

"Could it be my dead brother?" the father asked me over the phone. "He's been gone for almost forty years."

I met with the whole family at their home. The father was around sixty years old, and the "boys" ranged in age from thirty-five to twenty-one. In addition to the father and his sons, there was one very surly-looking ghost who appeared to be about eighteen or nineteen. I asked the father to tell me how his brother had died.

"He was just eighteen," he said. "I was twenty-one. We were drag racing and he flipped his car and hit a tree. I never should have let him try."

I noticed that the ghost was shaking his head in disgust.

"He always thought he could tell me what to do," the ghost spat out. "But I would have beaten him fair and square if he hadn't swerved and tried to run me off the road."

"He says you tried to run him off the road," I told the father.

The man's expression was pained. "I remember my car swerving," he said, closing his eyes. "I thought I was going to lose control, but I didn't. When I finally stopped, Joe's car was already wrapped around the tree."

He opened his eyes and looked right at me. "I never should have let him race," he repeated.

The ghost snorted. "You'd think he'd at least say he was sorry for killing his only brother," he said sarcastically.

It was clear that even after all these years, and even after the harm that the ghost had tried to inflict on the family, his living brother was still horribly broken up over his death. It was also clear to me that this ghost had such an attitude—so much resentment, and even hatred, for his brother and nephews—that he was never going to give up causing them trouble.

I went through my usual arsenal of arguments as to why he should go into the Light. But this guy was having none of it. And so I turned my attention to the family. Now, when I clear a house and am sure there are no more spirits present, I give the homeowners special quince seeds that are sent to me by my relatives in Italy. The quince is a fruit related to apples and pears. And to this day I don't know what my relatives do to these seeds, or how they energize them, but putting them up over doors will prevent a ghost from coming back into a space. It's also important to note that, by the same token, putting these seeds up while a ghost is present will prevent that spirit from ever leaving. The power of these seeds is not to be taken lightly. I'll tell you more about their use later in this book.

When it became clear that the vengeful teenager was not going to cross over, I pulled out the quince seeds and began handing them around like candy. "Carry them with you, like charms," I said. "They'll help protect you from his negative energy."

"You can't keep me away from them," the ghost shouted at me. "I'll ruin their lives, just like he ruined mine."

He was furious, but I just ignored him. I had raised teenagers, and I had a pretty good sense of what would happen next. In fact, I was actually afraid I'd start to feel bad for this kid, who was obviously bitter over having to watch his brother grow up and have the life and family he'd never gotten the chance at.

Shouting a string of unprintable expletives at me, the ghost flung open the front door and stormed out of the house. He slammed the door behind him so hard, it rattled the hinges. Let me tell you—we had those quince seeds up in every doorway of the house in no time flat.

Sometimes I wonder if he's still out there. He didn't seem like the kind of kid who would take my advice and try to find a funeral home where he could wait for a service and use the white Light to cross over on his own.

The White Light Exists for Everyone

The white Light is there for every creature—including animals—when life ends. Through my many years of working with the Light, I have come to appreciate its protective and benevolent powers. I believe that each time I release spirits into the Light, I am sending them on the next leg of a journey. Though I can never know for sure what kind of judgment or reward may await those who pass into the Light, I have come to believe that it's a powerful source of comfort to those nearing death. I know that spirits who cross over—become "of the Light"—are restored to their best selves.

I use the Light for a very specific purpose in my work and have taught my daughter Tara, who shares my ability to communicate with earthbound spirits, to create the Light, just as my grandmother taught me. I have never tried to cross over into the Light myself, mainly because I know that, as a living being, I do not belong there. I suspect that since the Light is an energy opening and I'm a solid mass, I wouldn't be able to enter even if I tried. Although I do not think the living can use the white Light to cross into a spirit world, I do believe that nearly everyone can access some of its protective and beneficial powers. In chapter 13, I will talk more about using the Light as a source of protection from harmful or negative energies.

4

WHY SOME SOULS
STAY BEHIND

And How I Convince Them to Cross Over

Your spirit is meant to go into the Light once it has left your body. All the earthbound spirits I've spoken to, from young children to the elderly, from college professors to folks who really weren't all that bright, know that the Light is there for them and that they can walk into it and join family members and loved ones waiting for them in whatever lies beyond this life. But knowing that they are supposed to take leave of this earth and move on to another existence doesn't mean that all spirits do it.

Each earthbound spirit is as much of an individual as he or she was in life, and most of them feel strongly about their reasons for not leaving. You or I might not agree with their rationale for staying, but when I talk to spirits who have chosen not to go into the Light, they clearly believe that their reasons for remaining earthbound are both logical and compelling.

There are many reasons spirits become earthbound. Most stay as a matter of choice, although some tell me that they had meant to go into the Light, but missed their window of opportunity and didn't know how to find the Light again.

Whatever their reasons, by the time I have finished talking with these earthbound spirits, most are ready to go willingly into the Light. It has helped that, over the years, I've developed a knack for helping to convince the less willing ghosts to depart. Often it just involves listening to their complaints or fears and offering some understanding and reassurance. There have been times when I've come home from clearing a house feeling more like a paranormal psychiatrist than anything else. Sometimes, however, I do feel it's in everyone's best interest to manipulate the spirit into leaving. With those ghosts who are reluctant to leave, whether they think they have good reasons to stay or are just plain ornery, I'll admit I've resorted to telling them what I think they want to hear to convince them to cross over.

At other times, my role has been to act as a mediator of sorts, conveying the spirit's wishes or grievances to different individuals and helping both parties—the living and the dead—come to an agreement that will let the earthbound spirit go into the Light at peace.

Over the years, I have convinced some earthbound spirits to let go of their attachment to a particular place or thing. I've reassured others that they won't be judged or punished and convinced still others that their presence is harming, rather than helping, those they love. I've talked to spirits who have stayed for revenge, for justice, or to protect a child or watch over other loved ones. And I've done whatever I've had to do to send some difficult ghosts into the Light when it was clear to me that their intent was to continue to stay and wreak havoc.

Despite the many ghosts I've talked to—and the many reasons I've heard for not crossing over—I honestly don't expect I've heard them all. All spirits have their own unique stories and rationales for not going into the Light when they first had the chance to do so. Following are a few of the most common reasons why spirits remain earthbound.

Attachments to Places or Things

Spirits will remain earthbound because they are attached to a place or a thing. I always think of these ghosts as being the people who never quite believed the famous phrase *You can't take it with you*. I'm often called in by families who suspect loved ones have stayed earthbound and want to know why. And frequently, I find that the recently deceased wanted to take precious jewels or items to the grave with them—explicitly stating that they wished to be buried wearing these items. Believe me, spirits do know if they're wearing their jewelry. If they are buried with particular pieces, I can see these necklaces, bracelets, rings, or watches when I'm looking at the ghost. Still, despite these clear instructions, it never fails that some member of the family, thinking that the dearly departed won't know any better, slips that diamond bracelet off Mom's wrist just before the coffin closes. You'd better believe that more often than not, if her diamonds aren't going, Mom's not going!

Other folks may have built a house and raised a family there, and now their spirits don't want to leave. Perhaps someone else cannot bear the thought of a life without his beloved sports car or her treasured piece of jewelry. Or maybe it's just that they don't want anyone else to get their hands on these things.

Attachments to Jewelry

One particular collector wreaked havoc on not just one, but two families when they came into possession of his prized antique watches. The funny thing about this story is that these families couldn't have been closer; if I had met them prior to the acquisition of the watches (and the attached ghost), I probably would have described them as the couples least likely to argue.

Donna and Stu Johnson were a brother and sister who grew up across the street from Jeff and Maureen Wilson. The four were fast friends, and no one who knew the families was surprised when Donna and Jeff and Stu and Maureen began dating in high school. Jeff and Stu went on to attend the same college. They graduated with degrees in engineering and found jobs in the town near where they had grown up. They married their high school sweethearts, and the foursome re-created their childhood by moving into condos across from each other. Donna and Maureen put their love of antiques and auctions to work and opened a consignment shop in a nice section of town. By the time the two couples were in their midthirties, they were financially comfortable. Each family had children, a boy and girl. Remembering their happy childhood living across the street, the four decided to keep their families even closer and bought a lavish duplex.

I first met Donna and Maureen when they called to ask me about some problems they were having in their shop. I visited and cleared the business of various ghosts who had been attached to furniture acquired at auctions and estate sales.

Donna and Maureen loved to go to the auctions. At one particularly high-end sale, they came upon a collection of Rolex watches that was being broken up and sold. A significant wedding anniversary was coming up for both couples (I'm sure you're not surprised that they married in a double ceremony), and each woman decided to buy her husband an antique watch. Although the bidding for the watches was spirited, they were able to get the two they had picked out.

The watches were only a few years apart in age, but were similar in appearance with only slightly different details. On the drive home, the women talked about how sure they each were that they'd bought exactly the right watch for their husbands. But then Donna mentioned that, although she liked her watch better, she actually preferred the box that Maureen's watch had come in. Maureen laughed and said that it was funny, but she preferred Donna's box. So they switched boxes. That night, after a group dinner, they gave their husbands the watches.

From that moment on, nothing went right in their homes. The building where they lived was a new one. It shouldn't have had all the problems it did, but they were relentless. The basements flooded, the furnace broke, and the ceilings developed cracks. It seemed as if their home was crumbling around them. As if that weren't stressful enough, the four friends started fighting. Things got so tense that the brothers and sisters moved in with each other.

Donna and Maureen were still going to the shop together, and one day it occurred to one of them that when they were in the shop, they weren't as angry at each other. I got a call from them that afternoon asking me if I thought they might have a ghost at the house.

That night I stopped by Donna's side of the duplex. Sure enough, there was a ghost going back and forth between the two homes. It was the original owner of the fancy watches. And boy, was he was a fussbudget! He told me about how much care he had put into his collection when he was alive. Now he was worried that his watches were not going to be happy if they were in different boxes.

"The serial numbers that match the watch are on the box, you know," he told me, wringing his hands.

I only wish all my cases were this simple to handle. I had the women switch boxes in front of the ghost. Then I made the Light, and he went right into it.

Attachments to Cars

Another type of earthbound spirit I frequently encounter is that of a man who just can't bear to leave his beloved car behind. I can't tell you how many times a widow, remembering her late husband, will say to me: "I swear he loved that Buick/Oldsmobile/Corvette as much as he loved me." I don't usually have the heart to tell her that her suspicions are completely correct.

I once got a call from a woman whose husband's behavior was driving her crazy. She suspected that he was having an affair and that he was, in fact, trying to drive her out of the house. She recounted several instances when—with her husband out of town—she'd hear banging in the garage and go downstairs to find the garage door wide open. Once, she'd found that the door that led from the garage into the house was unlocked as well. The last straw came when, after locking the house up for the night, she heard the banging in the garage and, frightened out of her wits, called the police.

By the time the police arrived, the house's burglar alarm had been activated and the woman was hiding in an upstairs bedroom. The police entered the house and called out to her. When she answered, they told her that her front and side doors had been unlocked, and the garage door was once again ajar. The woman's voice cracked as she told me her theory: Her husband was so desperate to take up with his mistress that he had given someone keys to their house so this person could spook her when he was out of town. I asked her if she really believed her husband would do something so cruel.

"That's what all my friends want to know," she said. "That's why I'm calling you. They think I have a ghost in my house."

It sounded to me as if her friends could be right. A ghost could certainly be responsible for the unlocked doors and misfiring burglar alarm—and also for her problems with her husband.

"It's like I don't even know him anymore," she said. "At first I thought he was having a midlife crisis. He went out and bought a Corvette convertible and started driving it every day. It seemed like all he thought about was that damned car. He even built a garage onto the house so the car would be sheltered. But now I don't think it's about the car. I think he's cheating on me. He goes out for long drives, and when he comes home he's edgy and mean. He'll pick a fight and then, half an hour later, he'll be just as sweet as he used to be. I really think he's trying to drive me crazy."

It was clear that this woman was at the end of her rope, but I didn't sense a ghost in her house as we talked. I did suspect that a ghost might at one time have been in the home; I could sense a feeling—a residue—as I spoke with her. In fact, by now I had a strong suspicion about what was going on in her marriage.

"Is your husband there now?" I asked.

"No," she said, her voice more angry than tearful. "He's out driving around in that damned car."

I told her I suspected that her problems were, in fact, related to an earthbound spirit, and asked her to call me back when her husband returned so I could check my theory. When she phoned back, sure enough, there was a male ghost in the kitchen with her husband. I told her I thought that the ghost was related to the car and asked her if she wanted me to come out to talk to him. She agreed.

When I got to their house, the husband and wife both met me at the door. The husband was a charming man, very relaxed and friendly. As his wife went to the kitchen to get us some coffee, he took me aside and explained that he'd do anything to convince his wife he wasn't having an affair; he was upset that she didn't trust him. "I swear, I would never see another woman," he told me. Then he gave me his version of events: He wanted to spend more time with his wife and had been trying to convince her to join him on his long drives, but she refused to have anything to do with his car. "She just hates it," he said, admitting that the bright red Corvette that was his pride and joy had become a huge source of tension between the two of them.

Although I was listening to him and nodding my understanding, I was also concentrating on the male ghost who stood just beyond him, in the doorway of the kitchen. He reminded me of a playboy from a 1970s movie: longish hair that curled up at his collar, a leather jacket over a white shirt unbuttoned halfway to his navel, and aviator sunglasses. I thought it was interesting how he had literally put himself between the husband and the wife.

"He feels the same way about the car as I did," the ghost said to me as the husband and I went past him to join the wife in the kitchen.

The three of us sat at the kitchen table while the ghost continued to lounge in the kitchen doorway. He was very chatty, and after a brief conversation I was able to confirm that this spirit was the one causing havoc in their home and relationship. The ghost told me that he had been the car's previous owner—and *his* wife had hated it, too. When he died suddenly, he'd been furious to find that the first thing his wife did was sell his beloved 'Vette. He was pleased that the new owner was lavishing such attention on the car, but he felt that the guy's wife was too much like his widow—she really didn't appreciate how a car that nice needed special care.

Even after I shared all this information with the couple, I sensed that the wife still hadn't fully let go of her conviction that her husband was having an affair. So I asked the ghost why he was terrorizing the wife instead of just enjoying his rides in the car with the husband.

"She was talking to a friend," he said. "And she said she was sorry her husband had ever bought the car. She was going to make her husband choose: It was going to be either her or the car. And I knew her husband would choose her. So I figured she had to go."

The woman's mouth dropped open. "I *did* say that to my co-worker." Then she turned to her husband. "Is he right?" she asked. "About what you'd choose?"

Her husband nodded and gave her a hug. When I asked if they were ready to release this spirit, they both nodded vigorously.

To tell you the truth, I expected that I would have some trouble convincing this ghost to cross over, especially after he admitted that he had, in fact, been the one opening the house and garage doors and setting off the alarms. That kind of interference with physical objects requires a tremendous amount of energy from an earthbound spirit. But I think he could see that despite his efforts, he hadn't succeeded in pushing the couple apart. Once I made the Light, he went peacefully enough.

I heard from the couple a few weeks later. They'd had a heart-to-heart and the wife had agreed to see if she could learn to appreciate her husband's fondness for the car. They'd just returned from a Corvette club rally and she admitted that she had really enjoyed the ride home—with just the two of them in the car!

Attachments to Places

Earthbound spirits may feel strongly about remaining in a particular place. And they can become very testy if "their" space isn't maintained to their liking.

A woman once left a message telling me that she was being haunted by a bed. Intrigued, I called her back. I was lucky to catch her on her cell phone. She was an interior designer, she explained, and was out looking for some pieces for a client. I couldn't sense an earthbound spirit with her at the time, but I was still curious to hear her story.

The woman explained that she had been looking for some antique furnishings for a client's home when she spotted a beautiful mahogany four-poster bed with carved posts and an old fringed canopy. "I had to have that bed," she explained. "Not for the client, but for me. And it's totally not my style."

After she'd brought the bed home and put it in her guest room, it became all she could think about. She'd be looking for wallpaper for a client, and realize that she was flipping through books thinking about what would look right with the bed.

Shortly after she bought the bed, she became obsessed with the fact that she'd left the matching dresser in the store. More and more convinced that the bedroom set needed to be complete, she returned to the antiques dealer, only to find the dresser had been sold. "I actually thought about tracking down the new owner," she admitted. "But I didn't want to feed this weird obsession I was developing."

Instead, she wallpapered the bedroom in a delicate floral print that she never would have chosen for herself. She bought a braided throw rug and a rocker and put them in the room. Still, she couldn't let go of the dresser. Several weeks later, she stopped by the antiques shop again—and there it was! The owner told her that the woman who'd bought it had been calling and complaining to him that it just didn't work with her decor, and purchasing it had been a terrible mistake. "He couldn't stand to listen to her complain anymore," the decorator told me. "So he bought the dresser back. I was so excited, I took it out of there that day.

"But here's where it gets really weird," she went on. "Now that the room is finished, I can't stand to be in it. Every time I try to spend time in there, I get a tremendous headache. Our houseguests all think the room is charming when they first see it, but they never have a good night's sleep, either."

Since we'd been having this conversation while the woman was in her car, I asked her to call me from her home so I could determine if there was a ghost there. In fact there was, and the woman immediately asked me to come over and find out what was going on.

When I arrived at her beautifully decorated modern home, I was not prepared for the tiny guest room tucked away on the third floor. The rest of the house was furnished with sleek pieces and bold colors. This guest room, with its sweet floral wallpaper, canopy bed, and ornate dresser and mirror, looked like it should have been in a 1920s home decorating magazine.

Though the style was a surprise, I wasn't all that shocked to see the ghost of a petite woman with her white hair pulled up in a neat bun sitting in the rocking chair. The ghost gave me a satisfied smile and looked around the room with a proprietary air. "I just *hate* what she did to the rest of my house," the ghost said. "But she's managed to decorate *my* room perfectly."

I asked the decorator if she knew anything about the history of her house. She explained that she and her husband had bought the home from the last surviving nephew of the woman who had been the previous owner. "We're only the second family to live here," she said. "You should have seen this place when we moved in . . . I had to gut the house and redo everything."

The ghost sat up straighter, gripping the arms of the rocker and glaring. I thought it best to change the subject. "Do you re-member what this room looked like?" I asked her.

"Oh, some kind of floral wallpaper," she said thoughtfully. "You know, I think I have an old photo album that the workers found when they were clearing things out. It had some photos of the house from the 1920s, '30s, and '40s." She left the room to get the album, and the ghost and I made small talk. She had been born and raised in the house, where she'd also died. Her nephew had inherited the home. Much to her disappointment, he had not moved in; he'd finally put the house up for sale after leaving it empty for nearly five years. The decorator and her husband had bought it and spent almost two years renovating before they moved in.

I asked the ghost what she had been doing for the past seven years. She told me she'd been hanging out at the neighbors' houses and visiting her own home as often as she could. She com-plained that those had been difficult years for her. She hadn't felt really happy in any of the other houses, but she didn't want to sit around in the shell of her former home.

"But after they started working on this house, I just felt so energetic again," the ghost said. "I'd follow her around whenever she came back to check on the workers. Sometimes I even went out shopping with her."

Once the new owners had finished their renovations and set-tled in, the ghost moved back in along with them. I realized that the constant stream of burly day workers and contractors had given this little old lady ghost some very strong energy—energy that she used to influence the homeowner whenever she could get near. Just like couples who've been together for decades begin to take on each other's likes and dislikes, or finish each other's sentences, ghosts who spend enough time with a person can use their energy to influence that person. This sweet little old lady ghost used all her energy to create the inexplicable decorating urges the homeowner had experienced.

The woman returned to the room with an old photo album. We

flipped through the pages, with the woman pointing out what work had been done in various rooms. At about the same time, we both noticed one particular picture probably taken in 1940. The woman gasped. The ghost smiled. Even I was impressed. The photo was of the tiny bedroom—and I am not exaggerating when I tell you that the room I was standing in was a picture-perfect re-creation.

It was clear to me that this ghost had never wanted to leave her home and had patiently waited until she could duplicate the place she had felt most happy. It took a little coaxing to convince her that she would be just as comfortable in the Light, but in the end I was able to release her, and the homeowner was able to redo the guest room in her own style.

Fear of Judgment or Punishment

I have talked to many spirits who did not cross over simply because they were afraid of what awaited them in the Light. Some of these fears seem perfectly reasonable. Ghosts whose lives were marked by violence or crime often fear a final punishment. Those who committed suicide or were highly religious and felt they had died without atoning for their wrongdoings also feared the judgment they might face. Often children will avoid crossing over because they are afraid they will "get in trouble" either for leaving their parents, or when they died with their parents, for not following Mom or Dad into the Light the first time.

It is these earthbound spirits, the ones who are filled with remorse or whose very human fears of the unknown prevent them from seeking peace, that I often find to be the most difficult to help cross over.

Suicides

Some time ago, I received a call from a woman asking me if I could help her find out if her father had remained earthbound. Ten years earlier, he had committed suicide, walking out of the family home and onto the ice of Lake Erie. He never came home.

Instead, the police found him close to the shore, frozen into the ice at his waist as if he had simply walked in and paused.

I could tell from the woman's voice that she was still distraught at the thought. "We were a happy family," she insisted. "My dad loved my mom and all of us kids."

Although she was calling me from her home, I couldn't detect a ghost with her, so I asked her why she thought her dad might still be around. She explained that because his death had been ruled a suicide, the priest from their Catholic church had refused to give him Last Rites. In the end, he wasn't even buried in a Catholic cemetery. "We went to church every Sunday," she said. "I worry that he's not at peace."

When the woman mentioned that her mother had died a few years after her father's death, I was sure I knew what she was hoping: that her parents were together again, and happy. I asked her if she or any of her brothers or sisters ever dreamed of their father. I explained that spirits who have crossed over often communicate with their loved ones in dreams.

"No one's ever mentioned it," she said. "And the six of us talk about Dad all the time."

I thought it was possible that her father had not crossed over. In my experience, suicides often fear they are going to hell and refuse to go into the Light. I asked her to contact her siblings and have each of them write a note to their father. The note needed to say that if he was around and wanted to talk, he should go to the woman's house on a certain day and time; I would call and see if he was there. Leaving a written note is the best way to pass a message to earthbound spirits. When you attempt to directly talk to ghosts, or acknowledge their presence, you can give them more energy. The more energy earthbound spirits have, the more they can influence you and your environment.

The woman did as I asked and her siblings all cooperated, though two of the five told her she was crazy. On the day we had picked, I called her house and immediately sensed the presence of a ghost. I described to her the tall, dark-haired man with a neat beard and bushy eyebrows who was standing in the room with her. The woman burst into tears. "It's Dad!" she said.

We arranged for me to visit her house, and I made sure she said the date aloud so her father would hear it. When I arrived at her home, the ghost of her father and three of her siblings were all waiting for me. This poor woman had been tormented by thoughts of her father's welfare for the past ten years, so I got right down to business, asking the ghost why he had committed suicide.

"I didn't," he said. "Not really."

He explained that he had fallen asleep on the couch one night, sheepishly adding that maybe he'd had one after-dinner brandy too many, when he thought he heard a voice calling from outside.

"It sounded like my mother," he explained. "So I got up and went out into the night. I don't know if I was sleepwalking or what, but I didn't take a coat or a flashlight or anything. I just walked out the door and followed the sound of the voice toward the lake."

He shook his head, as if still amazed at how foolish he had been.

"I don't really remember walking out onto the ice at all. But I do remember the sound of the ice cracking and the water. I remember thinking that the water wasn't as cold as I'd expected. That it would be all right to rest for a moment. It was like I went back to sleep."

He looked at his children, who were sitting in silence waiting for me to continue. "Tell them I'm sorry. I would never have chosen to leave them and their mother."

When I relayed this to his children, they looked relieved. But his daughter was still troubled. "Ask him if he's happy," she urged me. "Is he with Mom?"

The ghost shook his head, so I had my answer. Instead I asked him, "Why didn't you cross over?"

"I never had the Last Rites," he explained. "I didn't want to go to hell. And I didn't want to leave my family. It was really no choice: Go to hell? Or stay with my family?"

I asked the children if they wanted their father to cross over, and without hesitation, they all said they did. I told the ghost that he wasn't going to go to hell. We all knew he hadn't meant to kill himself, I said, and I could show him how to cross over. I made the white Light and told him to look into it.

"I can see my parents," he exclaimed. "I can see my wife!"

After he crossed over, the children all thanked me, especially the woman who'd called me in. "Thank you," she said. "Now all of us can be at peace."

While many spirits are afraid of meeting the unknown in the Light, I have also encountered spirits who have remained earth-bound because they knew exactly who they would come face-to-face with if they went into the Light.

I was called to the funeral of a man who had been a successful partner in a financial planning business. When I arrived at the viewing, I found his spirit to be very distressed. I asked him if he was ready to go into the Light.

"I'm not going there," he said to me. "I can see *him* in there."

I asked who *he* was: the other partner in the firm, it turned out, a much older man who had died several years earlier. I had been invited to his funeral, too, and knew that he had crossed over.

"Why don't you want to see Joe?" I asked.

The ghost told me that just before he'd died, he had received a visit from Joe. Apparently, after his death Joe would come back from time to time to check on his old company. Since he had crossed over, he was able to come and go without causing any problems, and the living partner was never aware of these visits.

Unfortunately, the remaining partner, once he had the business to himself, began siphoning money away from the firm. This enraged Joe, who knew the money should have been going to his heirs. Joe's spirit had managed to get into the dreams of his former partner. "I'll get you for this," he'd said. "I'll get even with you when you die."

"What's he going to do to me if I go in there?" the ghost asked me, peering into the Light. I told him that what Joe was going to do was maybe the least of his problems. He had to have courage, I added, and be man enough to admit his mistakes. But this guy was a coward through and through. No matter what I said to him, he would not go into the Light at his funeral home. I know for a fact that he had no intention of crossing over at all.

Some spirits I've met act as though they don't have a conscience and will trot right into the Light no matter how heinous their lives were. Others fear that one mortal sin is all it takes for them to end up punished for all eternity.

Seeking Revenge or Pursuing Justice

I often talk to ghosts who have stayed to seek revenge, and to the earthbound spirits of homicide victims who have vowed to bring their murderers to justice. It can be quite difficult to convince these ghosts to cross over. Most feel they have an important mission to fulfill; they don't want to leave until they've succeeded in righting the wrong they have perceived.

Seeking Revenge

A few years ago, an old man with a thick Slavic accent called me because he believed that "the spirits" had been sent to him by someone alive, to haunt and punish him. As I've mentioned already, I know from my own Italian background that such beliefs are not only common in the Old Country but often quite justified. As I spoke with this man over the phone, I could tell that there was indeed a ghost in his house, so I set up an appointment to meet with him.

The Slavic gentleman lived an hour or more away from me, in one of the wealthiest parts of Cleveland. His majestic home occupied nearly an entire city block, more a monument to his wealth than a place to live. When I rang the doorbell, a butler wordlessly answered, and I felt as though I'd stepped onto the set of some lush movie about the upper class in Europe.

I was ushered into a den. The old man was sitting behind an enormous desk in the center of a room filled with expensive, dark wood furniture polished to a high sheen. The eighty-year-old motioned for me to sit in a wingback chair across from him and told me his story.

He explained that he had been in the import-export business for most of his life, and it soon became clear that there was a shady element to his dealings. He not only referred to having been surrounded by "violent people" in his life, but hinted that he actually might have killed someone. Between the creepy, silent butler and the conversation, I found myself looking around the room for a quick exit should the need arise—which is when I saw the ghost. He looked to be about forty-five years old.

Before I could get the ghost's attention, he began shouting a litany of foul names at the old man, ending with a pointed "murdering son of a bitch." I was aware that the spirit was speaking a foreign language, but as I'd learned relatively early on, my ability to understand what ghosts are saying somehow transcends language. I don't have to communicate with them out loud; I sense and understand their words, as they do mine. It's hard to describe, but I can detect when spirits are speaking a different language because the words sound different—not so much accented as somehow vibrating differently in the air. It's another aspect of my abilities that I don't fully comprehend.

After he finished his rampage, the ghost turned his attention to me. "That kind old man," he began sarcastically, "murdered me. I was a professional arsonist, and I did a lot of work for him, burning down buildings." The ghost went on to explain that he'd tried to blackmail his employer for extra money; in response, the old man had had him killed. His body was thrown in an abandoned well on a deserted property, never to be found. Because the dead man had no family or friends, no one missed him, and a police investigation was never even opened. In response, his spirit hung around, determined to make the old man's life miserable, to make him pay for his crime. It had been twenty years.

"At first, very little bothered him," said the ghost, "but now he's getting old and he's starting to feel the pressure. I used to mess with the wiring, but now I've found that just yelling at him does more visible damage."

The old man blanched when I asked him if he'd been having trouble with the wiring in the house. He had. "Why did you ask about that?"

"Well, ghosts often affect wiring just by their presence, so it's a good clue that you might have one hanging around."

"That's true," the ghost chimed in. "Only once I figured that out, it was easy for me to hang around any frayed old wires and just wait for a fire to start."

"But in your case," I added, "the ghost knew this and was actually trying to start a fire. And if the house burned down, the fire department would have chalked it up to old wiring, never knowing who did it."

"How do you know this?" the old man asked, visibly shaking now.

When I said the ghost's name aloud, the old man went white as a sheet. The butler appeared out of nowhere and quickly gave the old man a few shots from an inhaler. When the old man was stabilized again, the butler straightened up and glared at me.

"How did you know that name?" he asked evenly.

"The ghost is standing right here, and he told me," I replied.

The old man composed himself. Showing a flash of the forceful personality he must have once possessed, he ordered the butler out of the room. He looked directly at me, his gaze unflinching. "So you know everything, yes?"

I just nodded.

"Tell him I'm not scared of him anymore," the old man commanded.

"He's a liar," the ghost sputtered.

"You can make him leave." The way the old man said this was less a question than a command.

"I can try," I replied, hoping that I really could convince this spirit to cross over. It wasn't an easy discussion, I can tell you that. But in the end, after telling a few silent lies assuring the ghost that he could become far more powerful and cause more harm from the next realm, he agreed to leave the house and the old man.

After I released the spirit into the Light, I gave the old man quince seeds and explained how he must put them up all over the house. The old man nodded and, satisfied that he had prevailed against his former henchman, rang for the butler. I was silently escorted to the door.

For a while, I watched the newspapers, curious to see if there would be any fires at the old man's house, but I never did see anything. And I really wasn't surprised.

Seeking Justice

As I've said, it is extremely rare that a ghost will seek me out. The only spirit whom I can remember coming directly to me was one who needed justice and knew immediately that I was probably the only person who could help him.

I had no reason to think that my night was going to be anything other than ordinary. Ted and I had gone to bed at the usual time. I'd read my book for a few minutes and then turned out the light. I couldn't tell you how long I'd been asleep when I suddenly awoke with the strong feeling that there was someone in the room with us. As a mom, I'd had this feeling before when my kids would wake in the night, creep into our room, and silently stand by my side of the bed waiting for me to wake up. Even though our kids were grown and living in their own homes, I guess my "mom-radar" was still working.

Opening my eyes, I was shocked—and honestly, more than a little scared—to see a man standing beside my bed. Ghosts rarely come into my home, so it took me a few minutes to catch my breath and whisper, "Who are you?"

"It's me. Sal. The DEA agent," the ghost replied.

I sat up and put on my glasses. I immediately recognized the ghost of the stocky agent with the graying crew cut. I had worked on a case with him and his partner about three years earlier. "Aw geez, Sal," I said sadly. "What happened?"

Sal was speaking quickly, like someone who knew he didn't have much time. "I was undercover and things went bad," he said. "Listen, Mary Ann, they're going to try to dump my body. I need you to call my partner so he can get there right away. Tell him where my body is. My wife—she's going to want it."

Then he gave me a couple of names. "Tell him this, too. Tell him I want these guys bad."

He gave me a phone number. "I've gotta go," he told me. "Please, call quickly." And then he was gone.

I glanced at my alarm clock: 2:30 AM. Telling myself that DEA agents were probably used to phone calls at all hours, I went to the kitchen to make the call so I wouldn't wake Ted.

"Hello, Dennis?" I said, when I heard a voice on the other end of the line.

"Who's this?" The man answering the phone didn't sound as if he'd been asleep. He sounded alert, and suspicious.

"It's Mary Ann. I worked with you and Sal on that case with the murder and the ghost."

"Why are you calling?" Dennis asked.

"Sal told me to," I said.

There was a long silence on the other end of the phone as Dennis worked out what that probably meant.

"Ah, hell," he said, sighing.

"Dennis, I've got to tell you some stuff from Sal. And he says you need to act fast." I repeated what Sal had told me: the location of his body, the guys he wanted Dennis to go after. Dennis read back the information, offered me a brusque "thanks," and hung up.

I stood there in the kitchen, staring at the phone. I hoped that Dennis would be in time and that Sal's wife would have her husband's body for the funeral. I hoped Dennis could find enough evidence to bring Sal's killers to justice.

I don't know how the whole story turned out. I know they got the body back, because I went to Sal's funeral; he was there, and he thanked me profusely. Whether his killers were caught and punished, I don't know. I watched the papers for a while, but I never heard from Sal again.

Staying to Protect the Living

Parents stay to watch over children; spouses stay because they overhear their survivors saying they don't know how they will live without their mate. Other spirits stick around out of the best of intentions. They may, for instance, feel the need to save someone from a bad habit, such as drug or alcohol addiction.

When I work with young married couples or young parents, I often come across the ghost of someone who clearly died before his or her time. I remember one young father who had died in a car accident insisting to me that he was not going into the Light. That he was staying to watch over his spouse and children. "Who will be like a dad to the kids?" he asked me. "What if my wife falls in love again?"

Whenever I come across spirits thinking along these lines, I explain the troubles they can cause by staying with the family. I tell them that, to show their love, they have to leave. Most of the time they listen to me and cross over.

Other times it's the older couples who can be stubborn—perhaps when an elderly husband dies, but his spirit decides to remain earthbound to take care of his wife. When this happens, you can expect that the surviving spouse will end up in poor health, maybe even in a nursing home.

It's also possible for living people to make a spirit feel guilty about crossing over. This is particularly true when someone has died quickly or unexpectedly. In one tragic case a young father had accidentally shot himself with his crossbow while out hunting. His wife was devastated. They had three children under the age of five and a four-month-old baby.

The man's sister had asked me to attend the funeral to see if the ghost could tell them what had happened. He confirmed that his death had been an accident. "I feel like such an ass," he told me, explaining how his bow had caught on a log on the ground and discharged an arrow right into his back. "I need to stay and make it up to them somehow."

I explained to him that if he remained earthbound, he would only end up causing his family trouble—he needed to go into the Light. But his wife, who was standing near the coffin, was sobbing and begging him not to leave her. I knew she was grieving, but I told her that it would not be good for him to stay. I told her how, even though he wouldn't mean it, his presence could cause chaos in the house and cause her or the children to be ill. Nevertheless, I left the funeral not knowing if he was going to take my advice and go into the Light, or listen to his wife's heartbreaking pleas.

A few months later, I got a call from the wife. "You were right," she said. "Everything is terrible. Can you tell me if he is still here?"

He was. When I arrived, he explained that he couldn't say no to his wife. She had begged him to stay, saying that she didn't care if she got sick or the house fell apart. But neither of them had considered what effect this might have on the kids. When his wife finally realized how detrimental his continued presence was, she was able to tell him that he could cross over, as painful as it was for her to release him. I made the Light and watched him go into it.

After he was gone, his wife asked me why I hadn't insisted that he cross over the first time. But as I explained to her then, and as I tell people now, I'm not the final word. I just give out the advice.

Busybodies Who Don't Want to Leave

Those nosy folks who just can't bring themselves to depart are perhaps the most harmless of all earthbound spirits—at least in terms of intentions. They don't mean to hurt anyone; they stay simply because they're curious. You know the type—the neighbor who is always peeking through your windows, the one who improbably shows up outside to water her gardens and chat every single time you pull your car into your driveway, the guest at the party who goes through the medicine cabinet. These spirits just can't believe they've been handed a free pass to snoop into whoever's life interests them at any given moment.

Of course, there are some with darker intentions. Stalkers may continue to haunt their obsessions—and as ghosts, they have access to many private moments. Jealous lovers can follow the love life of anyone they have left behind. Such ghosts may have a more negative impact than your deceased next-door neighbor who pops through to check out how you've redone the kitchen, or your interfering aunt Millie who rides along on your first date with a new love interest.

Many earthbound spirits have come to realize that they really don't belong among the living. And, especially if I catch them in some incriminating behavior, they are embarrassed enough to go into the Light without complaint. For those who pose a challenge, I sometimes threaten to put up quince seeds, thus trapping them in the same house for the rest of their earthbound stay. (It should be noted that I have never followed through on this threat. It would be a grave mistake to intentionally trap an earthbound spirit in any location. However, in the case of a perpetual snooper, the threat of confinement is an effective tool in convincing them to move on and cross over.)

Misconceptions About Earthbound Spirits' Abilities

I have talked to ghosts who stayed because they thought being an earthbound spirit would give them special powers. I don't know if they watched too many horror movies when they were alive, or what, but while being a ghost does give you abilities that the living do not possess, it doesn't give you superpowers.

Ghosts have told me they've stayed to give winning lottery numbers to their family members, and were sorely disappointed to find out that they had no way to control or predict lottery outcomes. If you couldn't pick the winning numbers when you were alive, you won't be able to pick them when you're dead, either.

The same is true for psychic powers. If you couldn't foretell the future when you were living, you won't have any better luck at it as a ghost. Ghosts cannot "control" human emotions, although most do use their presence (and energy) to manipulate the levels of emotion and tension in the living. For ghosts, it is easier to do things that cause negative energy, such as hiding important papers or jewelry, bothering pets, or otherwise encouraging tension. For most people, a stress reaction is an energetic reaction. It shouldn't be surprising, then, that as ghosts absorb this output of negative emotional energy, their own energy becomes negative. Simply being in proximity to an earthbound spirit can trigger a whole host of mental and physical reactions in the living. It's a vicious circle that is always good for the ghost and most often detrimental to the living person who is affected by constant exposure to the earthbound spirit's bad energy. With a few exceptions, ghosts cannot physically interact with humans; nor can they make themselves visible at will.

People's personalities don't change when they die. If they maybe weren't so bright when they were alive, they're no smarter as ghosts. Grumpy old men remain grumpy, bratty teens never grow up to be mature adults, and control freaks don't suddenly become Zen. In all my years of dealing with ghosts, I have come to the conclusion that the only way for spirits to evolve to higher levels than they knew in life is to go into the Light and experience whatever it is that awaits them there.

5

FUNERALS

Expect to Attend Your Own

MOST PEOPLE expect wakes, viewings, and funerals to be somber events. They know that these are times to offer, or receive, support from a community of family and friends who gather to remember the dead person and hold up the emotions of the living. For most societies, this ritual way of saying good-bye to a loved one is a chance to bring closure and a sense of peace to those who are still living.

My view of funerals and funeral homes is certainly different from that of most people. When I go to a funeral home, I'm expecting an interesting, sometimes wild, occasionally uncomfortable conversation with a ghost. The fact is: You can expect to attend your own calling hours and funeral. Remember that although the white Light is with a spirit from the moment it leaves the body, it will remain with that spirit for a few days *after* a memorial service. And it's rare that I've been called to a funeral home to find that the ghost wasn't also there. The one exception to this is when children die. I have never seen kids younger than three or four at their wake or funeral.

What Ghosts Do at Their Own Wakes or Funerals

When I walk into a viewing, I know what to expect. Although there have a been a few times when I've been memorably surprised—even shocked—for the most part, the behavior of the ghosts is very similar. As mourners approach the casket at the front of the room, they can see that the body of the deceased is laid out with the head to the left and the feet to the right. I see the casket and body as well, but I also see the ghost of the dead person standing at the foot of the casket. Of course, this makes perfect sense to me. In this position, ghosts are able to hear all the comments as the mourners pass by the casket. They can see how their hair looks, inspect the makeup job, and check out their outfit. Women, in particular, can be extremely critical about these three things.

Spirits also cruise around the room. They may listen in on conversations and admire the bouquets—while noting who they're from. Male ghosts like to glance out the windows, if they can, to count how many cars are lined up at the curb for the procession to the funeral service or cemetery.

Even when bodies have been cremated, spirits will still attend their memorial service. In this case, they usually stand to the left of the speakers. What I have noticed over the years is that as long as the family is following the deceased person's wishes about how the viewing, service, or burial should proceed, the ghost is content and will cross over into the Light—usually at the cemetery or right after the memorial service. It's harder on both the spirit and the family when someone's last wishes are not known. I've gotten as many calls from daughters who are distraught over what their mothers would have wanted to wear for the viewing as I have complaints from irate spirits who can't believe that the last outfit their friends will see them in is the hideous one their family has chosen!

In all my years attending funeral homes, I am still amused by how surprised the ghosts are when they learn that I can see them.

At one funeral I went to, the deceased was an impeccably turned-out silver-haired gentleman. His ghost looked so poised and elegant as he drifted around the room, admiring the flowers. His daughters had called me to the funeral because they had been unable to find his will or last instructions and were concerned by that lack of preparation and foresight—so unlike their meticulous father.

I slowly worked my way through the crowded room until I was alongside the distinguished gentleman. For a moment, I just stood next to him as he admired a particularly elaborate floral arrangement.

"Beautiful, aren't they?" I asked him.

He whipped his head around, startled. "You can see me?"

At first I thought it was kind of funny to see such an imposing figure at such a loss.

But when I nodded that, yes, I could see him, his composure cracked and I was shocked to see tears run down his face. "Thank goodness," he said. "I didn't know what was going to happen."

It turned out that the man's lawyer had taken advantage of the deceased's trust and friendship and had, shortly after the man's death, removed critical documents from the safe where they had been stored. The ghost told me that the lawyer was planning to falsify documents and redirect the dead man's estate into the business where he was the sole remaining partner. I was able to tell the daughters about their father's crooked partner and his role in the missing will. With the last of his business finally taken care of, the ghost was able to cross over into the Light after his funeral.

What I Do at Wakes and Funerals

Some of my earliest memories of talking to earthbound spirits are from when I accompanied my grandmother to funeral homes during calling hours. I'd talk to whatever recently departed neighbor or aunt or cousin might be present and answer questions from the large extended family gathered there.

I still go to funeral homes frequently, only now mostly at the request of strangers. In the old days, I would go to funerals if asked by any of my grandmother's huge network of friends from the Old Country. But these days, pretty much the only way I will attend a funeral or viewing is if an immediate family member of the deceased personally invites me. I won't go if a cousin or a distant niece or a well-intentioned nosy neighbor wants me there; I deal only with the immediate family.

The one exception I will make is when someone has suddenly died at the workplace. In these situations, I will talk to employers, and I'll go to the funeral home at their request. But I ask the ghost only one question on behalf of the employer: What is the password for your work computer?

Honestly, you would not believe how many people neglect to tell their supervisors the password for their personal office computer. And you might be amazed by how many computer techs can't access these personal accounts. But perhaps you wouldn't be surprised to hear how many times I've asked ghosts for a password, only to have them laugh heartily and ask me to pass an unprintable message along to their former employer.

I've done this enough to learn that most people aren't all that creative when it comes to choosing a password. When employers call to tell me that an older male employee has unexpectedly passed away and they need me to find out the password, I'll first give them a couple of the more common ones that I've heard to try out. My success rate with this approach is pretty good. You wouldn't believe how many men between fifty-five and sixty-five use *rosebud* as their password.

As I've become more recognized, especially in my hometown area, I've had to add a few other rules about funeral home visits. For instance, I no longer visit during the scheduled calling hours. If I try, all sorts of people—not just family members—realize who I am and want to know whether the dead person has any special messages just for them. With a crowd suddenly surrounding me, I then find myself in the awkward position of having to explain that I'm not there for a ghost chat, or to send messages back and forth from everyone who's coming to view the body. And on more than one occasion I know I have irritated the family priest or minister, who has arrived to lead the prayers for the departed soul only to find that the family has more interest in asking whether or not Dad likes his casket than they do in saying a rosary or prayer service.

And so I try to be very clear that, when I go to a funeral or viewing, I am there for the sole purpose of passing specific information along to the family. If a family wants me to come to a viewing and talk to a loved one, I try to schedule a time just after, or between, the scheduled calling hours. For many grieving family members, the first viewing is the hardest. After they have been at the funeral home for several hours, they can usually listen more calmly to what I have to say.

In other cases, when I know that the viewing is going to be crowded or traumatic—for instance, if a young person has been tragically killed—I agree to attend the wake, but I just slip into the funeral home as discreetly as possible and catch the spirit's attention. I can then ask the questions that the family wants answers to and meet later with the family members to pass these along. This is not the most satisfactory method, however, because even having the answers to a few questions can open up more unknowns. But in some cases it's the best I can do.

I think most people invite me to funerals because they really want to find out if the deceased has hidden money or jewelry or forgotten to tell them about something valuable. But the truth is, hardly anyone dies with millions stashed away under the floorboards. Others just decide to take their secrets to the grave with them.

Still, with as many funeral homes as I have gone to, you might think that I've seen it all. But I gave up that assumption years ago. Even though I've seen—and heard—a lot, I have no doubt that there are plenty of surprising situations I haven't yet encountered.

The Most Common Questions from the Living and the Most Common Complaints from the Dead

Despite the occasional shocking story from a wake or funeral, the people who invite me to a funeral home to talk with a departed relative fall mainly into a few basic categories. Oddly enough, the spirits I end up talking to at their funerals often have similar agendas also. And once a ghost discovers that I can pass on comments to those present, I usually hear the same litany of complaints and the same words of comfort.

Is There "Something" We Should Know About?

One of the most common funeral calls I get is from the person who wants to know if is there "anything" the deceased wants the family to know. (Translation: Where has Grandma stashed the silver and how can we get our hands on it?) Sometimes there really is money or jewelry tucked under the floorboards that the family was meant to have, and I can leave the funeral home knowing that family and ghost have exchanged important information. Other times, it's disappointing to see how upset the living can become when they realize that there is no "reward" for them once the funeral is over. Frankly, this type of greedy behavior can leave the spirit I am talking to pretty upset as well.

Nevertheless, there are times when people just have a sense that the deceased was troubled or there was unfinished business when they died. In these cases, the relatives who have called me usually find their instincts were correct. But that doesn't always mean that what they find out is what they were hoping for.

One woman, with her husband's permission, called me to her father-in-law's wake. There were three sons: a lawyer, a doctor, and an officer in the army. The youngest son, the attorney, had been the caretaker for his father during the man's last (and very difficult) years. His father had suffered a stroke, and the younger son, while a dutiful caretaker, was also resentful that his father's will evenly divided a substantial estate among the three brothers. He honestly thought that he was entitled to a larger share since he and his wife had let the father move into their home and had interviewed and hired a full-time caretaker.

Even though the father's speech was affected by the stroke, he was able to communicate with his son and others by writing or via computer. In any case, it happened that the father and the son he was living with had a huge fight. The other two sons sided with their father—which was probably easier, since he didn't live with them. Not long after that the father passed away.

The attorney's wife had called me because, despite her father-in-law's demanding nature, she had been fond of the man. And despite his speech impairment, she could sometimes understand what he was trying to get across. She knew that his nurse-companion, Daniel, could also understand the man's limited speech. And when she talked to the nurse after her father-in-law's death, he had seemed very uncomfortable. Daniel denied being told any deathbed secrets, but the daughter-in-law still felt that something wasn't right. Her husband, the attorney, had told her to go ahead and call me if it would make her feel better. As far as he was concerned, he didn't believe in any of what I did.

With this complicated history, I wasn't surprised to walk into the funeral home and immediately encounter an outraged ghost. This spirit wasted no time in telling me that after the disagreement with his youngest son, that son, being an attorney, had had another will drawn up. This version gave him a much larger share of the estate than his brothers—about 90 percent of all the assets. He waited until his father seemed to be failing, then, telling his father that the paperwork was intended simply to redistribute some stock allocations, had the man sign the second will.

"But I've outsmarted that scoundrel," the father's ghost told me.

In his last weeks, the father had asked Daniel to take him to another lawyer. He had never felt comfortable with this son handling his legal affairs, and the fight they had was the last straw. With the help of his nurse, the father had communicated to the new lawyer the terms of another last will and testament. This lawyer had been smart enough to have a doctor pronounce the old man in his right mind. The ghost was sure that the will was valid.

"Daniel knows where the will is," the ghost told me. "Go tell those boys to stop all this nonsense."

I looked over at the three strapping sons in the corner of the room. They looked like they were having an argument. As I walked over, I could hear the youngest saying, "Well, maybe he left everything to me because I took care of him all those years." His wife, the one who had called me, took me aside and asked if I could help settle the other brothers down. "They're very upset over the change in the will, as you might imagine," she said. "Did their father say why he did it?"

Can I tell you how awkward I felt at that moment? What was I supposed to tell this woman who had called me with the family's best interests at heart? That her husband was a liar and thief? That her father-in-law was still outraged?

Although I didn't want to drag him into the matter, I knew that the person they needed to hear from was the father's nurse. I called him over and gently told him that I knew he had something to say to the family. And then, as he began to talk, I rapidly excused myself. I may have been able to help the family find out the truth, but knowing it clearly wasn't going to make things any easier.

Are You Happy with the Arrangements?

I get a lot of calls from families concerned over whether the deceased is happy with the way all the arrangements have been handled. Sometimes they want to make sure that their cantankerous uncle George will promise to peacefully cross over; at other times, they genuinely wonder whether they have made their recently departed loved one happy with the choices they have made.

I have learned not to have any expectations of what I will find when I am called to a funeral home to answer this type of question. A while ago, a woman called to ask if I could come to the viewing for her husband. Her voice shook as she explained that she wasn't sure he'd be happy with what she'd done.

I arrived at the funeral home just before the first session of calling hours ended. There weren't many visitors, so I just signed the guest book in the lobby and continued inside. When I got to the viewing room, I have to admit that despite all my experience, I was stunned.

The man's casket was leaning straight up against the wall. It was tilted back slightly so that it didn't tip over, but there he was, standing straight up at the front of the room. His hands were folded across his chest; he was wearing a peaceful expression and a handsome dark suit.

I was so surprised that I didn't even look for the ghost. I just went right over to the widow and introduced myself. "What's this?" I asked her. "I can't believe the funeral home did this for you."

The woman admitted that she had gone to three different funeral homes before finding one that would accommodate her unusual request.

"But why?" I asked again. "Why is he standing up?"

The woman explained that her husband had been sick for some time and that in the final months of his illness he had said over and over again that he absolutely did not want a big fuss. No viewing, no big ceremony, no procession to the cemetery. He also told her that he didn't really trust her to follow his last wishes. He knew that ultimately she was going to be alive and he wasn't, and there was always the chance she'd do what she wanted anyway.

I still wasn't sure what was going on. But before I could ask her to be more specific, my attention was drawn to the ghost, who had circled back around the room and was standing near the casket. As I made my way toward him, I noticed that he was grinning from ear to ear. There was no doubt in my mind that the whole situation was making him very happy.

I glanced from the casket to the man and said, "Okay, this has me stumped. I hope you have some explanation."

His grin cracked into a laugh. He was enjoying himself so much that he didn't even seem surprised that I could see him.

"She never fails to amaze me," he said, nodding in the direction of his wife. "We've been married thirty-six years and I really thought that all those years she wasn't listening to me. But I guess she was."

At this point the suspense was killing me. "So what, exactly, did you tell her that your body ended up like this?" I asked.

"I told her that when I died, I didn't want to be laid out in a funeral parlor," he said, starting to giggle again.

"Okay," I said and waited for him to continue.

"That's it," he said. "Didn't you hear me?"

"Sure," I said. "You said you didn't want to be laid out—"

"You get it?" he interrupted.

I got it, all right. By now his widow had joined me in front of the casket.

"Did he tell you?" she asked. "Is it okay with him?"

I told him that her husband was more than okay with it; he was downright tickled pink. Not just because she had kept him from being *laid* out, but because after all those years, he realized that she really had listened to him.

There's One Last Thing I Need to Say

Sometimes the living feel they have something they need to tell the departed. This is usually some type of apology for bad behavior that occurred while their loved one was still alive. In this case, I don't always have to go to the funeral. I simply tell the worried mourners that when they get up to the casket, they should just whisper their apologies there. The ghost will be standing nearby and will hear them. I remind them that it's not enough to just think a sincere apology. Unless Aunt Florence was a mind reader when she was alive, she won't be able to tell what you are thinking just because she is now a ghost. For some people, this isn't enough. They want me to come to the funeral home to let them know if their apology has been accepted. I've learned to be very careful what I tell the living in these cases—I sometimes have to take into account what the ghost's motive might be in passing along certain information. I must try to understand as much as I can about both sides of any story before I share anything that could be hurtful to those who receive it.

I once was called to the funeral of a teenage girl who had been tragically killed in a car accident. Her parents wanted me to see if she could tell them anything about what had happened. She had been riding in the car with her boyfriend at the time, and although he had survived the accident he hadn't been able to give the parents much information at all.

When I got to the funeral home, I found a devastated family, a boyfriend clearly still in shock, and one extremely angry and vindictive teenage ghost. She was standing up by her casket, muttering about how her mother liked her to wear her hair pulled back but how she hated it that way and why did her mother get the final say? I tried a soft approach. "Maybe your mom wasn't thinking clearly," I said to her. "You can see how upset they are, still."

She whipped around and glared at me. "Yeah, well, what good is it being upset?" she said sullenly. "Besides, it's not like it was my fault I died. It was his." She pointed across the room at the grief-stricken boyfriend.

This was a pretty serious accusation, so I asked her for some more details. She went on and on, describing wild partying and irresponsible driving and illegal substances. According to her, it was her boyfriend who ought to be dead and she who should be sitting in the room full of mourners. "You tell them all that it's his fault that I'm dead," she demanded. "Tell them he killed me."

This is the kind of situation I hate: when I'm given information that I can't confirm and that might be harmful to the living people I share it with. The parents had asked me to see if I could learn anything more about their daughter's death. And now I had some very incriminating information indeed.

In this particular case, however, I was lucky. The town where the funeral was being held was one where I had done some work for a few of the local police officers. One of those officers had stopped by to pay his respects to the family, and I caught up with him outside the room where everyone was gathered. I told him he didn't have to give me all the details—I just wondered if there had been a toxicology report on the boyfriend.

The cop responded that the kid's blood work had come back clean. That, as far as anyone could tell, the girl had died because she wasn't wearing her seat belt, even though the driver was wearing his. He said that he was as sure as he could be that it was nothing more than a tragic accident. Suddenly, the ghost burst out into the hallway, clearly in search of me.

"You have to come in here and see what's going on," she said.

I followed her back into the room, and she pointed out her boyfriend, sitting and talking to several girls, probably her classmates. One of the girls reached over and patted the boy's hand as he fought back tears.

"You see," she fumed. "He'll have a new girlfriend in a few days. He'll forget about me, instead of remembering me forever." She abruptly changed gears. "Were you telling the cops what I told you?"

I had a flash of insight into her sad attempt at making her boyfriend suffer and suspected that maybe her information wasn't 100 percent true. I told her that I was going to check out everything she'd told me; if it were indeed true, I'd tell her parents. But since I suspected she was on a vendetta and might be the type to stay around and try to create more drama for the poor driver, I added that if she wanted her boyfriend to remember her forever, she'd go into the Light so that she could visit him in his dreams.

Well, someone must have told her boyfriend who I was—

because just as I was leaving, he asked if it was true that I had talked to his girlfriend. "She's here," I told him.

"Could you tell her something from me?" he asked. "Could you tell her that I'm so sorry that I didn't stop the car and make her put her seat belt on? She could be a drama queen and I didn't want to have a fight, so I didn't make her do it."

He was so stricken that I couldn't help myself from trying to comfort him. I told him that the police knew it was an accident; his girlfriend would have a chance to move on, and so should he. I could only hope that they both would take my advice.

Other times ghosts are the ones who have last regrets or something they need to say before they can be at peace. Of course, I don't really know how many spirits feel this way; it's not as if ghosts ask me to attend their funerals to pass along specific messages. Generally, spirits who feel that strongly about making something right are the ones who tend not to cross over. Still, there have been times when I end up feeling I've brought more comfort to the ghost than to the living people who called me.

An older woman had passed away after many years of ill health. Her daughters, who invited me to the funeral home, remarked upon how their mother had always seemed to be treating herself for some malaise or another, but they'd never really expected any of her illnesses to kill her. She had suffered from chronic fatigue syndrome, and in later years her doctors had diagnosed her vague aches and pains as fibromyalgia. The woman had ultimately suffered a sudden infection. Within a week, she'd become delirious from high fever; she then slipped into a coma and never recovered. Her daughters had listened to her incoherent mumblings during her fever and knew that she had wanted something specific done with the locket she always wore around her neck.

"We decided she should be buried with it," they told me. "But maybe she wanted one of us to have it? Or for us to share it?"

They described the locket as a gold heart that contained two little pieces of hair that their mother had clipped from their heads when they were babies. Both women were very concerned that they do the right thing with their mother's most treasured possession.

When I arrived at the funeral home, their mother was laid out in her casket with the locket around her neck. Her ghost was standing over the body, wringing her hands in despair.

"Did you want one of your girls to have the locket?" I asked as I stood beside her.

"I loved my girls and I loved my husband," the woman's ghost declared passionately.

I nodded and waited for her to go on.

"But the guilt. I think it was the guilt that made me sick," she said softly.

I have seen this happen over and over again. Once people are dead, they are willing to share things that they would never have revealed when they were alive. I don't always know whether they're simply unburdening themselves or are convinced that others should truly know, so I listen to their whole story before I say anything.

This ghost told me that before she met her husband, she had become pregnant. She had given birth and put the baby up for adoption. The baby's father, a soldier, had shipped out and never returned. Many years later, she learned that he had died. Several months after giving up her baby, she met the man who became her husband and went on to have two daughters with him. She never told him about her first child.

"The terrible thing was that the baby was adopted by people who lived in our town. I know who she is. Sometimes I would even see her. I thought about contacting her. But I never told anyone. Now I need you to do something for me," she said.

"Well, I don't know what good it would do to tell your husband now that you're dead. And your girls just wanted to know what to do with your locket," I replied. "Why complicate things?"

"Because they are complicated," she said. She told me that

although her daughters thought that the locket held two pieces of their baby hair, it actually held a piece of the woman's own hair and a curl from her firstborn. If she let them take the locket, they'd be living with her lies forever. What she wanted, she told me, was to get the locket back to her first daughter. "She needs to know I'm her mother," she told me. "I don't know why I know that, but she just needs to know."

I told her that I would do as she asked—but I'd have to tell her daughters right away so they could take off the locket before the burial. I added that I didn't see the need to tell her husband, though if the girls wanted to tell him it would be their business. She seemed to be fine with this and thanked me profusely.

Toward the end of the evening, the daughters, who had been grieving and meeting with visiting relatives, sought me out. They asked if their mother had anything she wanted them to know. We stepped into a private room, and I told them what I had found out. As expected, they both stared at me as if I were crazy when I told them the story. I gave them the name of the woman whom their mother wanted the locket sent to.

They really didn't say much to me at all. Just stared. I don't blame them. The news was completely unexpected. This was one of those times when I need to remind people that I am just the messenger. Of course I prefer it when I can say, "Yes, your mother said to tell you that there is twenty-five hundred dollars wrapped in the handkerchief in the bottom drawer of her bedroom dresser." But as I have learned time and time again, this is not always the case.

The interesting thing about this visit was that about six or seven months later, I was signing books after one of my talks when a woman I thought I recognized as one of the daughters approached. She gave me her name to put in the book I was signing. "Do you remember me?" she asked. "My mother was the lady who didn't want to be buried with her locket."

I told her I hoped things had worked out for her. They had, she replied. She and her sister were very happy they'd followed their mother's last wish. They had found their half sister and given her the locket. The three women had talked, and the two younger daughters had told her all about their mother. Their half sister had been extremely grateful, because she had been experiencing health issues and had no way to determine her genetic history. The two sisters, encouraged by this positive response, had also told their father, who was completely understanding about an event that had happened before he had come into the picture.

She thanked me again for passing on her mother's last words. "If not for you, we never would have met our sister," she said. "Mother would be so happy."

Did It Hurt? Were You Scared?

I've never heard a ghost say that it hurt to die. They've told me how much pain they were in when they were ill or became injured, but as far as actual death or dying goes—I can't recall anyone mentioning that it hurt. Others have admitted that they were scared, but more often than not I hear inspiring stories of the comfort that those in the white Light bring to the dead and dying who can see them.

One of my most moving experiences was attending the funeral for a soldier who had died in Iraq. Over the summer, we had lost over twenty young men and women from the Cleveland and Columbus area to the battles in Iraq, and each of the military funerals had been very rough. It had been difficult for me to find words to console the families who'd asked me to be there. The ghosts of the soldiers would tell me that they had died doing what they wanted to do. They were proud that they'd gone down fighting, and they were sorry if they had let anyone down. When I passed this on to the families, they were proud, of course, but not necessarily comforted.

But at one of these funerals, a young soldier, maybe twenty-two or twenty-three, told me something extraordinary. He was from a family of military men—from his great-grandfather to his grandfather to his father, right down the line. When I got up to his casket, he told me how sorry he was to be leaving his wife and his baby son. I replied that he would be able to keep a watch over them from the Light—he'd be able to get into their dreams and perhaps offer them comfort.

I asked him to look into the Light and to tell me what he could see. He stared for the longest time before whispering, "It's amazing."

I have heard spirits say this before, but I have never heard what he told me next.

"I see my grandfather," he said. "And he's not saying anything, but he's there and he's wearing his uniform. And behind him there are rows and rows of other people, all in uniform. And I don't think I know any of them, but they are all standing and saluting me."

I got the chills.

"I saw all the flags and the people on the route when they took my body from the airport to the funeral home," he added. "But now I'll be a hero when I go into the Light."

Later, when I told his mother about our conversation, a smile crossed her grief-stricken face. "Leave it to my father to come up with something to make everyone feel better," she said.

And I learned from that grieving mother, as I learn from every funeral I visit, that it is better to look for the good in everything. Otherwise, alive or dead, you will end up miserable.

6

MURDERS AND SUICIDES

When Spirits Stay After Unnatural Deaths

I MEET MANY earthbound spirits who died from murder or suicide. It's not surprising when you think about it: These are the ones who most frequently choose not to go into the Light. They stay to seek justice or revenge (in the cases of those that were murdered), or because they are afraid of what punishment might await them in the Light (in the cases of suicides). I have come across ghosts who've spent all the time since their death attached to the person who wronged them, waiting for their chance to even the score. I have also encountered spirits who found the attorney assigned to represent the criminal and did whatever they could—misplacing files, erasing phone messages—to disrupt the case.

When I talk to these earthbound spirits, they are usually incredibly grateful that I can hear them and relay their stories, whether to family members who need closure or to others, such as law enforcement officials.

Working with Law Enforcement

Because I do encounter earthbound spirits who are the victims of murder, I have developed working relationships with law enforcement officials both locally and nationally. The first time I encountered a ghost who had died as a result of a violent crime, I passed along the information to contacts in my local police department. A few detectives there were open to hearing about the ghosts of any murder victims I might come across, so I continued to share information with them. As a result, there were times when the police were able to use the information I gave them to make progress on open cases. Over time, certain officers would ask me to keep particular victims in mind in case I happened to run across them in the course of my work.

In fact, I still consult a huge file of more than two hundred cold cases that I got after I told the police about one particular ghost I encountered. She was a young prostitute—just nineteen years old—who'd been murdered by a violent john. I received a call from a local woman who was very concerned about some changes in the behavior of her two daughters. Both girls, who had always been very obedient and pleasant, had become rude and disrespectful. Having the ghost around them had influenced them as much as if they had started hanging out with the wrong kind of crowd. Their dress had changed as much as their manners: While they used to wear preppy clothes—neat jeans with sweaters or polo shirts in pretty colors—they now favored all-black outfits accessorized with torn fishnets. Without their mother's permission they'd acquired piercings and tattoos, and both had dyed their hair black. Not surprisingly, they had also started hanging out with a group of new friends whom their mother didn't approve of at all.

Perhaps today this manner of dress and defiance might be attributed to typical teen angst, but I met this family well before music videos promoted provocative dressing and goth was considered a fashion statement. There was no reason for their change other than the subliminal message they were absorbing from their exposure to this particular earthbound spirit's extremely negative energy. Their mother, suspecting that these drastic changes were more than teen rebellion, was unable to get through to her children and was at the end of her rope when she finally called me.

I went to the house to meet the two daughters. When I arrived, their mother ushered me into the living room, where the first thing I saw was about ten years' worth of school portraits of both girls lined up across the fireplace mantel. A few minutes later, the girls themselves came downstairs, and I have to tell you that if their mother hadn't introduced us, there was no way I would have picked them out as the same girls in the pictures. The older was about twenty, a college junior, and her sister was just finishing high school. They both flopped down in chairs across the table from their mother and me and stared in a challenging way.

I had just begun to ask the girls a few simple questions—Where had they been hanging out? Had they noticed any particular changes in their home?—when in waltzed the ghost of a petite young woman. She could have been really cute, except for the tough look on her face. When she spoke to me, her attitude was as hard as her expression. I wasn't surprised to learn that she'd been on the streets for most of her adolescence. Her mother had been an alcoholic with a series of abusive boyfriends who'd terrorized both the woman and her daughter.

I spoke to this tough little ghost for a while, and she finally ended up telling me where her body could be found (in an unmarked grave, because no one had ever claimed it), as well as how she'd died (beaten to death by a john). She added that she'd been dead for about five years and had spent time in the houses of several teenage girls.

"They're all so wholesome," she told me. "And wholesome just aggravates me."

I really wanted to convince her to cross over, since I could tell that she was still angry. I told her that no matter how many nice houses she went to, she was never going to get back her innocence. I looked over at the two girls, who were slouched at the table picking the black polish off their fingernails. "These two hardly look wholesome," I pointed out.

The ghost shrugged. "I guess I'm a bad influence."

I said that I could make the Light; she could cross over and maybe find some peace. I also told her that I'd pass on the information she'd given me, and maybe some of the people who had hurt her could be punished. This seemed to make her feel better. Since she didn't know the name of the man who had killed her, she gave me the name of the man who had been her pimp.

She did cross over, and the two girls gradually returned to their "wholesome" selves, much to their mother's relief. As I'd promised, I checked in with one of my contacts in the police department to pass along the information I had learned, including the number and location of the unmarked grave where the young prostitute's body was buried. The cop I talked to asked me for a description, and when I gave it to her, she pulled out a few sets of photos. I was able to identify one as the ghost, and the police confirmed that it matched with the grave number I had given them.

The strange thing was that over the next few months, I ran into a few more Jane Does in various houses. Each time I went back to the same detective with what I'd learned, and each time it checked out. That's why I now have a file full of unsolved cases from about 1981 through 1995. Since I received this file, I think I've run across maybe eight or nine of the girls. It's not many out of the hundreds of unsolved cases, but at least it's something.

That experience taught me that cops from all precincts talk with one another regularly—and also talk to officers from other towns and cities. And over the years, word has spread about cases that I've been able to help with. As a result, I have worked with local, regional, and national law enforcement agencies, and have contacts ranging from local cops to DEA and FBI agents. Of course, the information I learn from an earthbound spirit can't be used as evidence in court. Both the law enforcement agents and I are certainly sensitive to that.

The truth is, I have to be careful with whom I choose to share the information I gather from an earthbound spirit. I learned this lesson the hard way many years ago when I became involved in a case at the request of one of my local law enforcement contacts. The situation involved a nine-year-old girl who was abducted from her mother's car in a parking lot in an affluent suburb. The news hadn't made our local papers, so I wasn't aware of this particular event, but I had done some other work for a woman officer assigned to the precinct that was handling the case. She called and told me that although they didn't have a body, the evidence was indicating that the child was dead. If that was indeed the case, she wondered, did I think that the little girl would have crossed over?

I told her that if the child was dead, I seriously doubted she would have crossed over, given how distraught her parents were. Based on my experience, I guessed that if she was dead and hadn't crossed over, she'd be at home with her mother. But if they wanted to know for sure, the mother was going to have to call or meet with me.

I understood that arranging this kind of a meeting could be a very hard thing for a cop to do. To go to a victim's family and say, *Well, we've got this lady who can talk to ghosts* . . . I don't know what the police said to the woman, but eventually she agreed to meet with me. From our conversation on the phone, I knew that the spirit of the girl was there. So the girl was dead.

When I visited the house, the mother became very upset, and I left without really talking to her. But the girl was there, too, and I was able to get some information from her before I left. I gave the officer who had initially contacted me five or six pieces of information about the girl's death. The cop had already known two of them, but the others were fresh leads.

Shortly after this, the girl's body was found, and the FBI was called in to work with the local officers. I didn't think much about the case; unless the mother called me again and asked me to come and talk more with her daughter, I'd done all that I could do.

It was about a week later that I first saw the strange car parked in the cemetery across the street from our house. I don't know what made me take notice of it, but I soon realized that the car arrived each morning and stayed all day. This went on for several days. After a day or two, I noticed that the driver would get out and stand next to the car. When I realized that he had binoculars, I was totally freaked out. Give me a ghost any day over some Peeping Tom with binoculars!

I locked all the doors and picked up the phone to call my husband at work. I heard a series of clicks and figured the phone was out of order—not unusual with the phone service in our small rural town. When I finally got hold of my husband, he told me I was being paranoid.

That whole week I watched the guy, and he watched me. Early the next week, with the car still parked in the cemetery, I got a call from the suburban cop. She wanted to talk with with me privately. When we met, she immediately asked me where I had gotten my information about the missing girl.

"Everybody's really ticked off over at the police station," she told me.

"At me?" I asked.

"No, not at you," she told me. "Not exactly."

She continued: Her superiors had turned over the information I'd given them to the FBI official in charge. It turned out that the FBI had already possessed this information, but had withheld it from the local cops.

"So why are you buying me lunch?" I asked.

The woman lowered her voice. "I've got to tell you, Mary Ann—you're a suspect. You know too much. Don't be surprised if you're being trailed or watched, or if your phone has a tap on it."

Suddenly the clicks on the phone and the man in the cemetery made sense, and I confirmed my suspicions with the officer.

When all was said and done, I was under suspicion for about six months because I "knew too much."

I learned then and there that any relationship I had with a law enforcement agency would be a delicate one. These days, if an agency calls me and asks for my help, I do everything I can to assist. But I don't call them to volunteer information about every ghost of a murder victim I encounter. If I did, I'd be at risk of being lumped in with what many law enforcement officials consider "all those nuts." Or worse, I could again become a suspect.

It would certainly be easy if whenever a suspicious death came across a detective's desk, he or she could just call me up, drive me over to visit with the deceased's family, assume that the victim's spirit would be there, and wait until I could tell them everything they needed to put together an airtight case.

Unfortunately, it just doesn't happen like that. First of all, it can be awkward to suggest to a grieving family that I visit along with the officer assigned to their case—assuming that the victim even has a grieving family. There are plenty of John Doe or Jane Doe homicides that need to be solved, and I don't have the faintest idea where to go looking for these ghosts.

The next problem is that the only way earthbound spirits can tell me who killed them is if they know their murderers. If ghosts have seen their killers, I can get descriptions, of course, but it's not like I can ask the ghost to come on down to central booking and go through the mug shots.

Finally, any information that I pass along has to be carefully considered by those who receive it. If there is a chance of solving a crime, the law enforcement agents on the case need to be sure that they follow all procedures for obtaining evidence for the best chances of an airtight conviction. I realize that all I can do is tell them what I have been told. How they use that information within the scope of the law is up to them.

Staying to Seek Justice

In some cases, the ghosts of murdered people will remain earth-bound as they search for a way to bring their killers to justice. In these cases, the connection between victim and killer is often personal. In one case I worked on, the victim—Jenny—had called her sister only weeks before her death to say that if anything ever happened to her, the sister should let the police know that her live-in boyfriend, Connor, was responsible.

"I know Jenny didn't die of natural causes," the woman who called me said. "She was going to leave Connor and take their son with her. I know he killed her."

"What do the police say?" I asked.

The doctors at the hospital were saying that her sister died of a heart attack; pending completion of the autopsy results, the police were suggesting that perhaps drugs or alcohol were involved as well. But the woman assured me that, although Jenny had been a bartender, she did not take drugs and rarely drank.

When she told me that Connor's former wife had died of a heart attack, I thought the circumstances sounded suspicious. But I could also tell that the ghost of the dead woman was not with her sister. I suspected that she might be staying close to home, watching over her child, as the ghosts of mothers frequently do.

"I could come to her wake," I offered. But the woman told me that Jenny's body was still with the coroner in Denver, where she had lived, and that Connor was pushing to have her cremated and the ashes shipped back east to her sister.

"Don't you think that's odd?" I asked. "What about the police? If it's an ongoing investigation, they'll probably want the body intact."

The woman made it clear that the police weren't going to do anything further until they had the autopsy report. She didn't know if she could keep Connor from making final arrangements for Jenny's body.

I could hear in her voice that she didn't have the energy to keep fighting this much longer. I told her to get in touch with a detective, not a regular police officer, and to tell him or her everything she'd told me. And I advised her to do whatever she could to bring Jenny's body back home before it was cremated.

When the woman called me back a week later, she told me that her sister's body was at a local funeral home and asked me if I could go over and see if her spirit was with it. I knew the funeral director at this home, and it was easy for me to arrange a private time to meet with the woman there.

When we arrived, I wasn't surprised to see a ghost in the room with the body. But when I described the ghost to the woman, I *was* surprised to learn that it wasn't Jenny. I told the woman that the ghost was named Laura and that she had died about ten years earlier in a car crash.

"Laura was Jenny's best friend," the woman gasped.

The ghost explained that Jenny had stayed in Denver to be near her child. She didn't trust Connor with the boy. Laura's ghost had been with Jenny since her death ten years ago, and had come with the body as a sort of messenger.

Laura went on with her story: She had watched Connor use a medicine dropper to put something in Jenny's juice each morning for weeks. A glance at the label told her it was a slow-acting poison that could cause heart failure. "I tried to warn her . . . ," the ghost said helplessly.

Jenny's sister was sobbing, but I knew that we needed more information. I asked the ghost if she knew where Connor kept the poison. She gave me the name and address of a storage unit. I wrote it down and told the woman to contact the detectives in Denver with this information. I also told her to make sure the funeral director knew that the body would need to be autopsied.

Jenny's sister did as I told her and made sure that the coroner received enough tissue from the body to test for the presence of that particular toxin. Meanwhile the detective in Denver kept an eye on Connor and waited for the results.

Weeks later, she called me back to thank me for my help. The autopsy had come back listing cause of death as "suspicious." With Jenny's death now in the realm between natural causes and homicide, the detective was able to continue the investigation, focusing on Connor as a suspect.

Laura's ghost did not cross over. I suspected that she was going to go back to see Jenny, so I told her that she could go to a funeral home to find the white Light. And then she and Jenny could both cross over. With Connor under investigation, Jenny's sister was able to become the legal guardian of her nephew. She asked me to visit them at her home. Jenny's ghost was with her son, and once I assured her that he was safely in the care of her family, she thanked me profusely for all I had done. I made the Light for her, and she crossed over.

When Talking to the Dead Can Be Dangerous

I'm never afraid of the dead, but talking to the ghost of a murder victim in the presence of the living can be unnerving. I've learned that ghosts have nothing to hide. They will tell me everything. This is not always true of the living. If I'm talking to murder victims who know exactly how they met their death, and at whose hands—well, I can find myself in some very precarious situations.

In one of my most frightening and unusual experiences, the information given to me by a ghost triggered a confession from the murderer who, at the time, was sitting in the room with me, the ghost's widow, and other family members.

I'd had a strange feeling about this situation almost from the beginning. I had received a call from a woman who had been given my name by a counselor she'd been seeing following the death of her first husband and her subsequent remarriage. In our first phone call, she had told me about the unusual circumstances surrounding her first and second marriages.

To make a long story shorter, the woman—I'll call her Ellen— had grown up with two very different guys as her best friends.

The threesome, who referred to themselves as "the Three Mus-keteers," had gone to high school together and remained close after graduation. Pete had always been studious, and he attended a local college. Alex, a handsome boy with a troublemaker's repu-tation, became a plumber and continued his wild partying ways. Ellen became a beautician and found work in the town where she had grown up.

The three friends continued to hang out, but as time passed, Ellen and Alex decided that their attraction was more than friendship and planned to get married. "Pete told me he worried I was making a mistake," Ellen said. "He said that Alex was always going to be a drinker and a ladies' man and that he would break my heart. Pete was such a good friend, he always did watch out for me."

But Ellen was in love with Alex, so she laid down the law, and Alex swore he'd stop drinking and flirting. They got mar-ried and Pete was the best man. They hadn't been married more than six months when Ellen found out that Alex hadn't exactly been keeping his word. She read him the riot act, and even Pete stepped in to tell Alex to start acting like a real husband.

"Alex straightened up again," Ellen told me. "And we began to talk about raising a family."

Not long after that, Alex was killed in a horrible car crash. He and Pete had been coming home from a baseball game. They'd been drinking all day, and although Pete said he tried to take the keys, Alex had insisted on driving. Pete was thrown clear of the car and somehow, miraculously, survived, but Alex had been in the car when it plunged into a ravine and was killed.

"Pete and I really clung together in our grief," Ellen said. "And after a few months, I came to appreciate how steady and sup-portive he'd been. When he asked me to marry him, I felt like it was the right thing to do, to keep the three of us together somehow."

But Ellen hadn't been happy in her marriage to Pete and had sought help from a counselor to deal with the constant bickering and tension in their household. She was deeply depressed and suffering from physical ailments. She told the counselor that she worried she'd done the wrong thing. That she wanted to be sure that Alex would have wanted her to marry Pete. Along the way she'd been given my card. When she finally called, she admitted that she was hoping I'd be able to tell her if her first husband's ghost was still around her. She felt she needed some answers from him to get her life back on track.

As I spoke with her, I could see the ghost of a handsome, dark-haired man with bright blue eyes. I described him to her, and she was certain it was Alex. We made an appointment for me to visit her house and talk to him. Before she hung up, she asked if it would be okay to have Pete, her current husband, present as well. "I think it would mean a lot to Pete, to have Alex's blessing," she told me. I agreed and we set a date.

It was about two weeks before I was scheduled to visit her home when I got a phone message from Pete. He said he was sorry, but he and Ellen needed to cancel their appointment; they'd call back when they were able to reschedule. To me, the message had a *don't call us, we'll call you* subtext, so I crossed their appointment off my Saturday list and that was that. Or so I thought.

About three weeks later, I ran into the woman who had given Ellen my card. "Oh, I'm glad you're out of the hospital," she exclaimed. "We were so worried about you."

I had no idea what she was talking about and told her so. "Ellen told me that you had to cancel your appointment with her because you'd been rushed to the hospital for emergency surgery," she explained. "I hope you're feeling better."

I corrected the woman, telling her that I was in fine health; that, in fact, it had been Ellen's husband who'd canceled our appointment. Now it was her turn to be puzzled. She said she'd let Ellen know about the miscommunication and hoped that we'd be able to get together.

Obviously I was intrigued when I got a call from Ellen a few days later. She was calling from her office, apologetic about the mix-up. She had no idea why Pete would have left such a message, she told me. In fact, they'd recently been at a party where someone had told them how accurate my information about one of their relatives had been, and both she and Pete were eager to reschedule.

By now, my radar was up. I suggested that maybe Ellen invite Alex's siblings to join us as well. If there was something weird going on with Pete—whether he had decided I was a fraud or whatever—I felt I would be more comfortable with a few other people around. We made an appointment for a week later.

No one called to cancel this appointment. When I showed up at the house, Ellen, Pete, and Alex's two brothers and sister were all waiting. Alex's ghost was there, too, and it didn't take him long to fill me in on what he so desperately wanted someone to know. When he told me what he knew about his death, I could feel the chills march up my spine. I knew—without anyone saying anything specific—that I was sitting in the kitchen with the person who had killed Alex. And I had no idea what the heck I should do about it.

Ellen was asking me to ask her dead husband all sorts of questions: "Why did you get behind the wheel when you were so drunk? Why didn't you let Pete drive?" And the ghost was shaking his head at each one as if to say *No, no, no* . . . Everyone was staring at me, waiting to hear what he had to say.

Finally Pete spoke up. "Maybe he's saying something that we should hear in private. Maybe you and I should go into the other room. You can tell me and then I'll break it to Ellen."

Stalling for time, I sort of nodded and said that well, yes, that was one possibility. I asked Ellen if she wanted me to just let Pete know and then he could tell everyone.

Ellen immediately protested that everyone in the room loved Alex and that everyone deserved to hear what he had to say.

By this point, Pete was sweating and pale. I looked straight at him and said, "Well, Alex is telling me that he understands how things might have ended up the way they have, and that he's happy you've tried to comfort Ellen." I said a few more generic things that Alex had told me, and then I continued.

"You know, Pete, Alex has some very specific things he wants me to tell you. He's wondering why you were buying so many rounds that day when the two of you went to the ball game. He says that it wasn't like you to drink so much. You need to come clean with him."

Pete stared ahead blankly for a long minute and then said, "He's told you everything, hasn't he?"

I just nodded.

Putting his head down on the table and beginning to sob, Pete confessed to killing his best friend. He'd gotten him drunk on purpose, he admitted. And then, on the ride home, when Alex passed out, without even thinking about it Pete slipped out of the driver's seat. He pushed Alex behind the wheel, slipped the car into drive, and let it roll down into the ravine. He'd jumped down after it and blacked out. The next thing he knew, he was in the hospital and Alex was dead.

I cannot even describe the mood in the room. All I can tell you is that I couldn't get out of there fast enough. I made the Light for Alex, who crossed over immediately. Pete went to prison, and as far as I know he's still there. It's one thing to hear ghosts tell me who killed them; it's another thing entirely to have the murderer confess to my face.

Suicides

While spending time in the company of murder victims can be upsetting, and talking to these spirits about who killed them and why can be unnerving, I find it much more disturbing to spend time with the ghosts of people who have killed themselves. There are some unique situations that surround the spirits of suicides.

I frequently run across the ghosts of people who committed suicide many, many years ago. Often these people were Catholics and killed themselves knowing that their church considered it a mortal sin and believing that their souls were doomed. Their expectation was that they would go straight to hell. They often tell me that they remained earthbound because they feared that there would be no forgiveness in the Light. For them, the risks of staying on earth as ghosts seemed less than the risks of going into the Light and facing certain harsh judgment. When I encounter such spirits today, I can explain to them that the Catholic church now regards suicide as the act of a mentally ill person; they needn't fear going to hell. Once I tell them this, they are usually grateful for the opportunity to cross over.

But as times have changed, the reasons for not going into the Light seemed to have changed as well. I have noticed an alarming trend among many suicide victims, particularly in today's younger generations. These days, when I come across ghosts of folks younger than fifty or so—and especially teenagers—who have committed suicide, I am meeting spirits who are not remorseful in the least. They have no fear of punishment and were not apprehensive at all about what would happen to them after their death. For these spirits, suicide is often an act of revenge or spite, rather than despair. This is a unique group of spirits in that they may or may not decide to go into the Light. But their decision about whether or not they cross over is not based on any fear of judgment or a sense that they will be punished. Instead, for these disaffected souls, it is as if being dead is just another new experience. And some tell me that they are planning to stick around for a while to see what it's like. Others imply that maybe being dead isn't as interesting as they thought it would be and that maybe going into the Light will provide them with the new kind of experience they seem to crave. I'm not sure what this attitude says about our current generation, but I do know that it can make dealing with the ghosts of suicides rather challenging.

Perhaps because of my experience in talking to people who are dead, I get a fair number of calls from living people who want to know what would happen to them if they were to commit suicide. My answer is always the same: "I can't tell you. I don't know."

What I *can* tell them is that often, when I encounter ghosts who died by suicide, they tell me that at some point they tried to stop the process, but it was too late.

It's interesting to me that people who commit suicide may want to leave this world, but they do not always simply cross over into the next. In some cases, this can mean that there is more to the suicide than meets the eye. In many suicides, I am invited to the funeral because the family has unanswered questions—no matter what someone may write in a note, many more questions always seem to remain for those who are left behind. Often families are angry and want to understand why loved ones would kill themselves.

I've also had the police contact me to help them investigate murder-suicides, or suicides that might have been murders, or murders that might have been suicides. Of all the ways to die, taking your own life can create the most dramatic ripple effect. However, people who commit suicide are generally doing so for selfish reasons and usually aren't too concerned with the mess they are leaving behind for others to sort out.

In one particularly unusual case, a man's apparent suicide created an unbelievable tangle for all those who knew him. The police called me in to help when their investigation of the death hit a dead end. The man's wife was saying it was suicide, but evidence at the scene had suggested that there might have been someone else involved. The police had a main suspect—and a good reason to believe he might have been involved in the crime—but their suspect had a rock-solid alibi.

What made this case so unbelievable was that the suicide victim was a twin—and that twin brother was the main suspect. The dead man's wife had told the police she was positive her brother-in-law had nothing to do with her husband's death, despite the fact that his lighter was found on the floor of the garage, right under the dead man's feet. The police, however, had the lighter, and the fact that the victim had died by hanging with his feet bound but his arms free, and no sign of how he'd managed to get himself to the high rafters of the garage. They also told me they knew the wife had been having an affair with her brother-in-law; the husband had most likely found out.

Armed with these facts, I visited the crime scene, but there was no sign of the ghost. The wife and the dead man's twin brother were equally adamant that he had killed himself. They were as willing to have me talk to the ghost as the police were. Based on some information the wife had given me, I suspected that her husband's ghost was still around, so I arranged to meet with everyone at the home the couple had shared.

The detectives, the wife, the twin brother, and I all sat at the table and waited. The tension was unbelievable. The detectives glared at their main suspect. The widow and her brother-in-law exchanged furtive glances and tried to hold hands under the table. I just wished I were somewhere else. Finally the ghost came into the kitchen. I acknowledged him and let him know that I could see and talk to him. Then I got right to the point. "So, who killed you?"

The ghost, by this time, at least had the good sense to look dismayed by what he had done. He shuffled his feet and looked around nervously as I waited patiently. "I killed myself," he finally admitted.

"He says he did it himself," I told the group at the table.

"How?" they all asked in unison.

As the ghost explained what he had done, it became clear that it had been his intent to frame his brother for his death. "I knew they had started an affair," he said. "And at first I wanted to kill her . . . and him, too. But then I thought that I might as well just kill myself, and maybe, just maybe find a way to hurt them the way they hurt me."

He'd left his brother's lighter on the ground and thrown the noose up over the rafters. Then climbed up and shimmied across the beams to the noose. Sitting up on the rafters, he bound his feet with tape, tied one end of the rope securely to the beam, slipped the noose around his neck, and simply jumped off.

"I guess I don't hate either of you enough to let them think it was you," the ghost said to his brother. "But I do still hate the both of you. It wasn't worth killing myself over, I see that now."

When I told him that I could make the Light and let him go to a more peaceful place, he couldn't wait to leave. To me it was as if he were stomping out of the room and slamming the door behind him.

Even when folks think they are doing the family a favor by ending their lives, it can result in pain and misunderstanding. Some time ago the adult children of a mother and father who had died in a double suicide pact invited me to their parents' funeral. Unbeknownst to any of the children, their father had been diagnosed with an inoperable brain tumor. Knowing how short his time was going to be, he and his wife made elaborate arrangements to commit suicide. The wife went through the house and cleaned out all their possessions. She sorted them into piles to be given away and set aside special things for each of their four children. They organized all their financial concerns and prepaid for their funeral, right down to ordering the flowers. They left a long and detailed note for the children, explaining what they intended to do and why.

And then—and this is the part that amazes me to this day— they went out to their backyard, where the husband had rigged up a very complicated system with his shotgun. With the wife facing her husband, he managed to fire the gun so that the single bullet passed through his wife, killing her, and then lodged in his heart.

At the funeral, the kids were struggling to understand. They wanted me to ask their parents why they had done what they did. Of course I felt bad for the pain the children were experiencing. Yet when the ghosts explained to me why they had chosen to end their lives as they had, and I saw how bewildered they were that all their careful preparations weren't more appreciated, I could almost understand how they'd thought they were doing exactly the right thing.

No matter how many spirits of suicide victims I have talked to, I still find it hard to comprehend what might drive people to take their own lives. Some situations I can empathize with more than others: cases of terminal illness or unremitting pain or mental illness that causes profound despair. But again, for every tormented spirit I talk to who has seen suicide as the only way out of tremendous mental or physical pain, I'll meet another ghost who has inexplicably chosen to die simply to spite someone.

In case of unnatural deaths, whether by murder or suicide, I never know what I will learn in my conversations with these earthbound spirits. I don't know if there will ever be a time when I am not amazed, shocked, or outraged by what I learn. In these difficult cases, I am often most deeply affected by the impact murders and suicides have on the living—on those who are left to sort out the reasons and details and secrets behind these deaths. And I try to do what I can to help these often troubled spirits obtain justice, repair misunderstandings, or explain their incomprehensible actions.

7

CHILDREN

How Young Spirits Are Different

CHILDREN ARE remarkably in tune with the world of spirits that surrounds us. My experience has taught me that most living children are able to see or sense earthbound spirits, as well as spirits who have crossed over into the Light, and even guardian angels. The information about ghosts that comes from children living in houses inhabited by earthbound spirits is usually consistent and reliable.

After I reached the conclusion that children have an innate and intuitive ability to connect with spirits, there was a period of time when I did wonder why it was that I can see and communicate only with earthbound ghosts. What I've finally decided is that at some point in my early childhood, I too must have been able to see other kinds of spirits. Since it was so easy for me to communicate with earthbound ghosts, though—and because my grandmother believed in and nurtured my gift—I believe I simply developed one ability to the exclusion of others.

In retrospect, I was incredibly fortunate that my grandmother was so encouraging about what I was doing. Most children who claim to see imaginary playmates are told to hush, to stop imagining, to grow up, to act like a big boy or girl. When people ask me about whether or not children can see spirits, I now tell them that experience has taught me that imaginary playmates are not always imaginary, and children chatting away at a tea party for invisible guests may actually be talking to spirits only they are aware of.

It's also clear to me that as children grow up, and well-intentioned adults praise the traits of practicality and reason, imaginary playmates are forgotten. I cannot recall having any ghost playmates, and I suspect that most adults would be hard-pressed to remember any invisible friends from their childhoods.

I do, however, remember the first child ghost I ever saw. I was in third grade and rode the bus every day with a girl named Lucy. Lucy got on the bus at the stop after mine and got off right before me each afternoon. One afternoon, as the bus began to pull away from the curb, the driver suddenly slammed on the brakes and began screaming. I can remember looking out the window and seeing Lucy lying on the sidewalk. I can even remember thinking, *Why is she doing that?*

When I got home that afternoon, the phone rang almost constantly. My mother told my sisters and me that Lucy had been hit by a car and killed as she crossed in front of the bus. The next day at school, the nuns began morning prayers by having us pray for Lucy's soul. The nuns also took our whole class to Lucy's funeral Mass. Lucy's ghost was there, sitting in the pew next to her distraught parents. I can remember trying to catch her eye. I wanted her to know I could see her. But she never even glanced in my direction. We weren't allowed to go to the cemetery, so I don't know if she crossed over or not.

I still remember how frightened some of my friends were about going to Lucy's funeral. They were afraid to look at her coffin in the front of the church; they were afraid of all the grieving relatives who filled the pews. I knew what to expect since I had already gone to a lot of funerals with my grandmother. But at those funerals, all the ghosts I had talked to had been strangers. This was the first time I had known the person who had died, and it made a strong impression on me. As a result, I firmly believe that parents should take their young children to calling hours and funerals, especially to those of people the children are not emotionally attached to.

It's important for children to realize that the dead are not frightening, and that while the bodies may have closed eyes, the deceased are not asleep. Making this distinction will, in fact, help children with any fears they may harbor that being dead is somehow like being asleep. Parents need to help their children to understand death is part of a process. While people are sad to lose their loved ones, the person who is dead is not someone to be feared.

After Lucy's funeral, I remember asking my grandmother why I didn't see ghosts of babies or younger kids. She told me it was because children have guardian angels, and guardian angels take their spirits to heaven. Because my grandmother didn't have the same ability that I do, I know now that she was telling me what she believed to be true, but it was many years before I felt I really understood the unique way in which children, both living and dead, navigate through the spirit world.

Infants

I have never seen the spirit of infants at their memorial services or funerals. And I'm really not surprised. After all, what does a baby know about such things? There's just no need for them to be there. Along the same lines, there's nothing that an infant's ghost would be able to tell me, since infants don't communicate verbally. Nevertheless, I did wonder about what happened to the spirits of infants when they died. Obviously, since I don't see them, they must cross over, but I always wondered how. It was only after many years of attending funerals and visiting people's homes that I was able to answer this question to my satisfaction. I remember, quite vividly, one encounter that helped define my perception of what happens to an infant's spirit after death.

It was a night in late summer, and my husband and I had returned home late after a dinner party. Our two girls were sleeping over at their grandparents' house. As we pulled into the driveway, I could hear the phone ringing inside the house. I dashed in and managed to catch the call. It was one of the officers from the state highway patrol. I'd worked with him before, and he didn't waste any time with pleasantries.

They had a "situation" on their hands, he said. There had been a crash involving a family from out of state as well as the son of a prominent local family. The boy was already on the way to the hospital and three members of the family were dead, with the fourth in very bad shape. Could I come right away?

The night had cooled and a thick fog had come up, making driving very hazardous. Although I'd been nervous on the drive home from the party, I knew I had to get to the scene quickly. My husband turned the car around and about twenty minutes later, we were pulling up to the scene of the accident. It was horribly sad. The ghost of the father, who had been driving, was standing next to the ambulance as his wife was being loaded. He was cradling a child in his arms. It was clear that the ambulance would be leaving in a matter of minutes, and I knew that the distressed ghost would want to follow his wife to the hospital.

I went straight up to him and said, "I can see you. I need to know what happened here."

The ghost was dumbfounded. "You can see me?" he repeated.

"Yes, I can. And you need to tell me what happened so I can let the officers know," I said urgently.

He told me that he was sure, absolutely sure, that he'd been on his side of the road. It had been so foggy that he'd been using the shoulder as his guide. It was a winding country road and he wasn't familiar with the area, so he'd been navigating by keeping the passenger's-side tire on the dirt shoulder. He couldn't remember seeing lights or hearing brakes screeching. All he could tell me was that the children were nearly asleep, strapped into their car seats, and his wife had just unbuckled her seat belt to turn around and comfort their younger child, who had started to fuss when he dropped his pacifier.

I looked at the child in his arms. It was a little girl, maybe fifteen or sixteen months old. And then I realized he'd said *children*. "Where is your other baby?" I asked. The ghost gestured with his head to a spot just behind him. When I looked closely, what I saw was so strange that I couldn't believe I hadn't noticed it as soon as I arrived. I guess I had just been so intent on getting whatever information I could get from this family before they disappeared that I had failed to notice the spirit of a tiny baby—maybe two or three months old—that was floating in midair slightly behind the father's right shoulder. As far as I could see, there was no one holding the child.

Nevertheless, I couldn't see the baby's face. It was as if he were being held against someone's shoulder. "Who's holding the baby?" I asked the father, as casually as I could.

"My grandmother," he replied.

I asked him how long his grandmother had been dead. He told me about twenty years, but oddly, she appeared younger than he remembered her looking when she had died. In fact—and he was quite specific about this—he recalled that she had suffered from a dowager's hump, which had left her stooped and twisted. "But she's standing perfectly straight and holding the baby now," he told me.

As we were talking, the baby slowly rotated down and around until he was lying as if cradled in his grandmother's arms. Now I could see his face and see that he looked like he was still sleeping contentedly. "Thank you," I said out loud, not knowing if the spirit would hear me. The baby shifted again, and was once more upright, cuddled against his grandmother's shoulder.

Once I saw that the baby's spirit was peaceful, I turned my attention back to the father. "You understand that you and your children are dead, right?" I asked.

He told me that he did, but he was worried about his wife.

The paramedics were telling me they were ready to go. I pulled one aside and asked him if he thought the woman was going to make it. I could tell from the look on his face that he didn't have much hope for her. As the paramedics closed the doors of the ambulance, the ghost of the father grew agitated. "What will happen to her?" he asked me.

I told him I didn't know. I added that he could leave both babies with his grandmother; she'd take them into the Light. Since I expected that his wife would soon die, too, I suggested he go with her to the hospital. If she died, they could go into the Light together. "You'll see your grandmother there with the babies," I reassured him.

In another case, I visited a hospital where a mother and an infant were both on life support. When people are on life support or in a coma, their spirits are still with the bodies. When a person is brain dead, the spirit leaves the body. In this case, the infant didn't have any brain activity, and the hospital staff were getting ready to disconnect the life support once her father returned to the room.

The woman's mother (the baby's grandmother) was the one who had called me and was in the room at the time I arrived. When I saw that the spirit of the infant was again seemingly cradled midair, I immediately asked her whether the child had another grandparent who had died. The woman told me that all of the baby's immediate family was still living. Again, though, it was clear to me that a spirit I could not see was taking care of the baby. Since it was not the spirit of an immediate family member, I like to think that my grandmother was right—the baby's guardian angel had arrived to take her into the Light.

Toddlers and Young Children

In more than fifty years, I have encountered only four or five ghosts of children who were under the age of five, and all of them were very articulate. One of the most interesting encounters

I have had with a child ghost was with a three-year-old spirit whom I encountered almost by accident.

I had been asked to visit a house by a family who was experiencing some serious problems. The woman who called me sometimes did tarot card readings and, to my surprise, had not taken any steps to protect herself or her family from the spirits who might arrive along with some of her clients. The family also had a teenage daughter with some mental health issues, who had begun complaining about the voices she heard that were planning to "get her." The family had a terrible time with anything mechanical. Their cars would break down, the furnace in the house seldom worked correctly, and the electrical system was totally unreliable.

When I arrived at the house, I wasn't all that surprised to discover a powerful negative energy creating a disturbance, but I was a bit startled when I saw a very young girl spirit quietly sitting in the living room. By her clothing, I could tell that she had died quite some time ago, probably in the late 1930s or early 1940s.

I guessed that she was about four years old, but when I asked her how old she was, she held up three fingers. She was incredibly articulate for such a young child and was able to tell me her story pretty clearly. She spoke with an accent that I recognized as German. I asked her how she had come to live in the house. She told me that her mommy and daddy had sent her to America to live with Aunt Esther, Uncle Harry, and cousin Betsy, but Aunt Esther was mean, and even though she said that her mommy and daddy would come soon, they never did.

I asked her how she died, and she told me that she had gotten sick after eating the peaches that came in the glass jar. Aunt Esther gave her the peaches every morning in her oatmeal, she continued, and one day her tummy just hurt and hurt. Even though the doctor came, she started to cough up blood. After that, she said, her tummy didn't hurt and Aunt Esther didn't talk to her anymore.

When I asked her what became of her aunt and uncle and

cousin, she told me that she had stayed with them until her cousin Betsy became older and started to ignore her just like her aunt had. Then she had just found children who looked nice to her and followed them to their homes. Whenever they got bigger, she moved to another that she felt comfortable in.

"But there are no children in this house," I pointed out to her.

"I know," she told me. "But here, for some reason, I can play with the toys they have for the children who visit. It's fun."

I asked the woman who had called me if she kept any of her daughter's old toys in the house. She explained that she did have a collection of toys, but they were all new. They were for her grandchildren, who visited often. "I hate these electronic toys, though," she complained. "I can't tell you how many times I'll come into a room to find them turned on. No matter how many times I replace the batteries, the silly things always seem to malfunction."

I glanced over at the little ghost, who grinned and said, "Sometimes I like to make them all go at once."

I don't know how this ghost got the energy necessary to turn on electronic toys, but I suspect it had to do with the chaotic atmosphere in the house: the negative energy, the emotional energy from the teenage girl, and the energy from the stream of tarot card clients.

In my opinion, the house was no place for child, even if she was a ghost. I made the white Light for her and told her that if she walked into it, she'd be able to find her mommy and daddy and everything would be okay. She looked at me suspiciously, and I can't say I blamed her; I think her short life had been a hard one, and she didn't have much reason to trust adults. But she did go into the Light, and she never once looked back at me.

By the time children are five years old, it is more common for me to see their earthbound spirits. I suspect that this is because, by five years old, most children can understand their parents' grief. They may listen to a parent who says, "Don't leave me." Or, like many children of this age, these young spirits may simply decide that they're going to do exactly what they want to do—and if they want to stay with their families rather than cross into the Light, that's exactly what they're going to do.

Of course, these young ghosts do not grow older while they are earthbound, and so many, many years can pass in which they're forced to move from house to house in search of a place where they feel comfortable. The fact is, anywhere there are children, there are likely to be the spirits of children. Whether they're alive or dead, kids like the company of other kids. It is so easy for a ghost child to follow a family home from a petting zoo or story hour at the library, or even from preschool. Just think like a five-year-old: "There's a pretty mommy and a little girl; I'll bet they have a lot of toys." Or "Oh, look, that daddy and his boy have a nice dog in their car." The next thing you know, your house is home to another child.

While children may try to go back to their homes or families, often the circumstances around their death cause them to become disoriented or afraid; many will avoid going into the Light or actually flee from familiar places. Once they've become confused or frightened, it is difficult for these young spirits to find their way back home. They simply become accustomed to spending time in homes or with families that feel comfortable or familiar.

I had a very dramatic encounter with a young girl ghost who was eight years old. Ted and I had been spending the holidays with a friend who lives on a vast ranch in Arizona. As you approached the main house, you passed through an impressive wrought-iron gate decorated with folk art figures of children at play. When we first arrived, I noticed a ghost of a young girl playing with the sculptures on the fence near the gate.

I mentioned her to our host, who was familiar with my work. He told me she might be the child of one of the ranch's employees, who had tragically died a few weeks before my visit. He asked that if I saw her again, I talk to her and see if I could find out anything to tell her grieving mother.

A few days later, I was sitting on a bench in the courtyard enjoying the sunshine and a fountain that was home to a school of koi when I saw the girl shyly lingering by the fountain. She had a spooked look, and I knew from my foster parenting that some kids are uneasy around adults. I suspected she was one. I also suspected that she thought that, just like all the other people on the ranch, I had no idea she was there.

I began talking aloud to myself. "I love that pretty yellow fish," I said. "I wonder what his name is."

"Goldie," the little ghost whispered.

"I like that name," I said, looking at her for the first time.

I was afraid she was going to run away, but instead she moved closer to where I was sitting. "I've named them all," she told me.

"What's your name, honey?" I asked.

"Becky," she whispered.

We talked about the fish for a while, and then, as casually as I could, I asked her where her mommy was. I expected she would tell me that she was somewhere nearby, at work in the main house on the ranch.

"I don't know," she said.

After a few more gentle questions, I learned that she wasn't related to anyone at the ranch. She told me she had been "hit on the head by a man"; when she woke up, the room was hot and dark and there was fire everywhere. She had seen the white Light, she told me, and she'd seen her older brother go into it, but she didn't want to follow him. All she wanted to do was to get away from the strange house she had been staying in. I felt strongly that this little girl's violent death had not been an accident. As I tried to get more information about where she had lived and how she'd found her way to the ranch, I saw our host walking toward me. Although I tried to wave him off, it was too late. The ghost had vanished.

I told him what I had learned and what I further suspected. He knew my track record in working with law enforcement, so I wasn't too surprised when, that night before dinner, the sheriff—

Buck—stopped by the ranch. Our host introduced me as a friend from Ohio and invited him to join us for a cocktail. "Thanks, but I can't drink on duty," Buck said. Then he swept his cowboy hat off, gave a little bow in my direction, and said "Howdy, ma'am." For a minute I felt like I was an extra on the set of a Western movie.

The owner of the ranch asked Buck if he'd heard of any recent deaths of children in a fire. Buck said that yes, in fact, he had an open case where two children had been killed in a suspicious fire, and why were we asking? I figured I might as well speak up. I asked him if one of the dead children was named Becky Gonzalez.

Buck gave me the suspicious look that I was more than familiar with. I see it often on the faces of law enforcement officials when I give them correct information about a confidential case. "How do you know her name?"

"I asked her," I replied.

Now I could see that Buck was trying to figure out how to be polite to the nutcase from Ohio staying at his friend's ranch. I figured it couldn't get any worse, so I added, "I can see and talk to people who have died."

Buck sat down hard and looked at his friend. "I think I'll take that drink," he said.

I offered to get more information and see if I could help his case. After talking to his friend and me a bit longer, Buck agreed that he'd be back the next day to find out if I'd learned anything else.

Luckily Becky walked right up to me the next morning as I sat throwing toast crumbs to my friends the fish. I managed to find out that she had two half sisters and a brother. She and her siblings had lived with her mother and her stepfather the next county over, maybe a hundred miles away from the ranch. Her biological father, who was being sued by his ex-wife for child support, had taken her and her brother to his home, which was in the same county as the ranch I was staying at. He'd set his house on fire and killed them.

Becky told me that she had made her way to a library, where she remembered her mom had once taken the kids for story hour. There she'd seen a little boy—Jackson, the grandson of the owner of the ranch where we were staying—and had followed him home. Jackson and his parents lived in their own house across the road from the main house, and Becky was very happy playing in their yard and visiting the goldfish.

I did help Becky to cross over. I made the Light and told her that she would be able to find her brother if she went into it. Before we left Arizona, Buck came by the ranch to let us know that they had a solid lead. The police had been looking hard at the girl's stepfather, an ex-con, but had not been able to get any breaks in their case. When they shifted their focus to Becky's biological father, they began to uncover some incriminating information. They thought they would be able to issue a warrant for his arrest shortly and expected that they would be able to convict him for the murder of his two children.

The saddest cases I've seen in my work, however, have not been children who choose not to cross over, but parents who refuse to let a beloved son or daughter go into the Light. In one tragic case, a mother's desire to keep her son close to her after his death was so strong that she was actually able to sense his presence and, on some occasions, feel his touch.

I had received a call from the woman's mother, who was distraught at her daughter's actions in the months following the death of her young son. The boy was nearly five when he died and had been the light of his parents' lives. They were an older couple who'd had a very difficult time conceiving. When Joey was finally born, they were ecstatic. To their horror, he contracted a rare form of childhood blood cancer, and they did everything in their power to get him healthy. It seemed as if the chemo and the transfusions were working, and Joey was in remission, when suddenly the cancer returned and he died.

At first, the mother's grief was immense. She told her parents and her husband that she was never going to let Joey go. As most people would, they believed she was referring to the memory of her son, but soon her behavior became so irregular that her husband moved out. She told her mother that she could feel her son snuggling with her in bed at night, that he still played in his room, and that she would kill herself if he ever went away.

Her mother was naturally distressed and called me to see if I could tell her whether the boy's ghost was indeed still at home with his mother. I really wanted to help this family. I told the mother that, if she could get her daughter to call me from her home, I would tell her if Joey was still there and help her talk to him.

It took some time, but one day I finally got a call from the mother, Mindy. She started by saying that she didn't need me to tell her if Joey was still with her; she knew he was. And she was right. As I spoke to her on the phone, I could see a thin boy with short brown hair and big blue eyes. I described the yellow plaid shirt he was wearing, and Mindy started to cry. "He loved Bob the Builder," she explained. "He always wanted to wear that shirt and pretend he was doing construction."

Mindy decided that she did want to talk to Joey and invited me to her house as soon as possible. Given her obviously fragile state, I asked her to have her mother present as well. I didn't really know what to expect when I arrived, but the home was tidy and well kept, with Joey's room just as it must have been when he died. In contrast with the neatness of the rest of the house, there were trucks and toys spread all over the floor. I asked Mindy why she left the toys out, and she explained that Joey still played with them each day. Again, she was right. I watched as Joey's ghost skidded into his room, flopped down on the floor, and began pushing one of the dump trucks around while making truck noises.

What was so interesting to me was that, although Mindy could not hear or see Joey, she talked to him as if she knew he could hear her. "Go ahead, go jump on Mommy's bed," she told him. And he jumped up and sprinted down the hall and was soon bouncing on her bed and grinning with glee. Mindy lay down on the bed and said, "Come snuggle with me." I watched as Joey stopped bouncing and curled up next to his mother.

"He's right here," she told me, pointing to a spot at her right side.

Joey was, in fact, curled up right where she was pointing.

Although I knew that having Joey cross over would be the best thing for both mother and son, at that moment, I honestly did not know how I was going to convince either of them of that fact.

I began by asking Mindy if this was what she wanted for her son: to remain eternally a four-year-old, never moving on. Was this really what she thought was best for him?

And what about for her, I continued. Did she want to be a mother to a four-year-old for the rest of her life? I told her that if Joey went into the Light, he'd be able to come to her in her dreams and communicate with her in ways that he was unable to do while he was earthbound.

Mindy just looked at me and asked, "Can't he stay with me until I die?"

Unfortunately, I find it very hard to lie when I am asked such a direct question. I had to admit that he could. But I couldn't promise that he would. "Kids are curious," I told Mindy. "And there may come a day when he leaves and, for whatever reason, can't find his way back. I can't just go out looking for him. He'll be gone forever. Until he crosses over, you won't know where he is or what he's doing."

From the look on her face, I knew I'd made some progress. She wasn't ready at that moment, she told me. She wanted to keep Joey with her a bit longer. I told her that when she was ready to let him go, she could call me. I'd come and make the Light for him.

About a month later, I got a call from Mindy. She thought she might be ready, but for one thing: Who was going to take care of

Joey in the Light? I asked the usual questions about whether or not any family members had passed away, but Mindy said that Joey didn't know any relatives who'd died, although her own grandmother was in the hospital and very ill. "Could Grandma take him?" she asked me.

I told her I thought that was possible, and so I waited again for a call. Two weeks later it came. Mindy's grandmother had died. I told her to tell Joey to get in the car with her and meet me at the funeral home. Of course, Grandma's ghost was there, and once I explained the situation to her—and told her how worried I was that Mindy would change her mind—she agreed that she would take Joey with her and cross over right after the end of calling hours. I stayed until the end of the calling hours and watched as Joey, happily holding his great-grandmother's hand, walked into the Light with her.

Teenagers

Oh, boy—teenage ghosts. I could write a whole book on these particular spirits. The most important thing to realize about teenagers, living or dead, is how susceptible to influence they can be. Parents often tell me about sudden troubles or changes in behavior that they've noticed in their child. When this happens, I pay particular attention to the adjectives they use to describe their teen: *moody, sullen, self-conscious, sarcastic, smart-mouthed, insecure, cliquish, clannish, mean-spirited, unpredictable, emotional*. By the time the exasperated adult is finished describing the teenager, I usually have an excellent idea of what type of ghost I am going to find when I visit.

Teenagers are more likely to experiment with devices and activities that can invite spirits into a home. Sleepovers where the Ouija board came out, or séances held while Mom and Dad were out to dinner, have resulted in more calls to me about earthbound spirits than I can count. A typical session of Ouija board play might attract the earthbound spirit of a teenage girl, for instance,

who would then seek to draw enough energy by influencing living teens to spread rumors about a member of the group or make
another girl self-conscious about what she wears. In what would
be a nightmare scenario for any concerned parent of a teenage
girl, a sleepover séance or Ouija board outing might attract the
earthbound spirit of a teenage boy. I know from experience the
havoc that such a situation will wreak.

In one disturbing case, a teenage girl who had attracted the
earthbound spirit of a guy in his early twenties during a Ouija
board session became so enamored with the idea of a spirit "boyfriend" that even after I sent the punk into the Light, it took
several weeks for the girl to get over her "breakup" and return to
her normal, upbeat personality.

Teenage boys aren't as likely to play with Ouija boards, although the rise in popularity of movies and TV shows about the
spirit world has encouraged teens of both sexes to experiment
with magic and exploring the spirit world. The earthbound spirits
of teenage boys act just as you'd expect teenage boys to act. They
particularly tend to hang around at gyms or sports complexes,
where there is a tremendous amount of energy both from the athletes and from the air of competition during games and meets.

As a result, these young spirits can have a lot of vitality. They
may be able to manifest some physical actions that would be difficult or impossible for other types of spirits.

In one instance, the ghost of a teenage cross-county star took it
upon himself to give his home team an advantage during a particularly grueling season. I had gotten a call from the wife of a coach
at a high school in a nearby town. She told me that her husband
had been complaining nonstop about problems in the gym: missing files in his office, unexplained computer glitches, and, most
of all, weird occurrences out on the cross-country course. During
races, it would appear that someone had moved the directional
arrows or placed hazards such as rocks or tree branches in the
middle of a previously cleared course. After hearing one of my
talks at an Ohio venue, she had decided to call and see if I could

tell her whether it was an earthbound spirit making her husband's life so miserable.

Luckily her husband was at home at the time of the call. I was able to tell her that, yes, her husband did have a ghost attached to him—a gawky-looking teenage boy. Although her husband told her he thought she was flat-out nuts, he agreed to humor her by letting me come out to their house and see what I could learn from the ghost.

When I arrived, the coach, his wife, and an anxious-looking teenage ghost were waiting for me. Before I could start to ask any questions, the ghost stuttered, "Could you tell Coach that I'm . . . I'm really really sorry about what happened with the guy and the ravine."

He did look pretty sheepish. So I immediately relayed the message. Now, this coach was a real *don't-mess-with-me* type—the kind of guy who has no problem keeping fifteen or twenty teenagers in line. But when he heard what the ghost had said, he started to look a little edgy. "You're not from around here," he said to me. "And we made sure that particular incident didn't get much press. How did you know?"

I sighed to myself and told him exactly what I tell everyone else who asks me that question: "The ghost who's standing right here in your kitchen just told me."

Meanwhile the ghost was really squirming. "I thought it would help the team if I switched some of the course signs around. Maybe get the other team disoriented. How was I supposed to know that some transfer student was going to be running for our team that day? Stupid doofus fell right off the cliff and broke his leg. Coach was pretty mad. I guess the kid was some hotshot record holder that Coach personally recruited."

I asked the kid if he'd been responsible for the missing paperwork and the various electrical malfunctions in the gym. He admitted that he had. At first he wanted to get Coach's attention so he'd notice how he was helping the team. And then, after the incident on the cross-country course, he wanted to get his attention to apologize.

Meanwhile, the coach was still staring at me as if he was trying to figure out who on the team might have tipped me off. So I asked the ghost for more information. Personally, I wondered why he was hanging around with an adult, instead of with some kid from the team. I found out that he had been dead for nearly eight years and didn't know any team members anymore. He'd been a runner himself on the track and cross-country teams at the school.

When I told the coach the ghost's name, he immediately called up a teacher who'd recently retired from the high school. I listened to the one-sided conversation—which consisted mostly of the coach offering the kid's name and then saying, "Uh-huh. Okay. Well, then. Hunh. Okay. Thanks."

When he hung up, he just looked at me and said, "Okay, then. Ask him to please tell me where he put that missing paperwork."

I got the answers, then offered to make the white Light for the ghost to cross over. I think that the poor kid was so embarrassed for making trouble for the team and for basically cheating to help them win over the past few years that he was happy to go. He was really a pretty good kid, I think.

The coach's wife called me a few days later to let me know that the paperwork was exactly where the ghost had said it would be—and the team had won their meet that week.

Even though the ghosts involved may not mean to harm anyone, I cannot stress enough how dangerous it can be when teenage ghosts mix with living teens. A lot of car accidents that involve teenage drivers also involve the influence of teenage earthbound spirits. I'm not saying that joyriding teenage ghosts are going to grab the wheel or step on the gas pedal or brake, but if they're in the car with you, they can be a distraction. It's important to remember that these spirits are drawn to similar teens with high energy. These ghosts have the ability to do a little more than other earthbound spirits simply because they have so much energy to draw on.

It's easy enough to protect vulnerable teenagers from the influence of spirits: Just have them carry a quince seed along when they leave the house. You can get charms with these seeds, or simply tuck one in a teen's wallet or purse. The protection offered by these seeds (which are the same ones I put up in houses from which I've cleared spirits) can keep a teen—or anyone—from picking up one of the earthbound spirits who hang around malls, gyms, skate parks, movie theaters, or any other high-energy spot teens love to frequent.

8

ANIMALS

Loyal After Death

WHEN IT comes to the behavior of animal ghosts, I'm still learning new things. I do believe that anything living has a spirit, and that any creature with a spirit has a white Light that comes to it when it dies. Although my grandmother never talked to me about the spirits of animals, over the years I have seen the ghosts of both domesticated and wild creatures. As a pet owner, I've also seen the spirits of many of my own animals. And from these various encounters, I've begun to understand more about what can compel an animal spirit to either go into the Light or choose to stay earthbound.

After an animal dies, I suspect that its spirit has about the same amount of time in which to cross over as a human spirit, but I don't know for sure. It may be that some have less. When my beloved African pygmy hedgehog Pinda died, I could see her spirit for the first few hours after her death. Actually, that's how I knew she was dead. I walked into the room where I kept her aquarium and saw Pinda scurrying around on the carpeted floor. I wondered how she'd managed to knock the top off her home, but when I looked closely, I could see that the screen was undisturbed and Pinda's body was curled in her sleeping spot. After a few hours, Pinda and her Light were gone.

Like human ghosts, the earthbound spirits of animals rely on energy from living sources and can cause disruptions and inconveniences to the creatures around them. But because domestic animals are generally rather small, the amount of energy their ghosts need and the type of influence they can have is also less than the energy and influence of human ghosts. I have seen the ghosts of larger animals, such as horses or moose, and I can guarantee that just as you would most certainly notice if a horse or moose were to get into your home, you *will* notice the effects of its earthbound spirit's presence.

Compared with the human spirits I notice or interact with on an almost daily basis, I really don't encounter that many animal ghosts. I've seen a ghost cow. I've seen the spirits of fox and moose and elk in the wild. But in general, most of the animal spirits I encounter are those of pets. This makes perfect sense to me, of course. Wild animals are not easily seen when they are alive. It's instinctive for them to hide when a human is in their environment. And just like the ghosts of humans, the ghosts of the animals I have encountered behave as the animal did when it was alive.

Unfortunately, I'm not Dr. Dolittle. I can't just talk with these animal ghosts when I see them, as I can with human earthbound spirits. Everything I know about animal spirits has been learned from observation and the interactions I have had with different animals over the years.

Nevertheless, as far as I'm concerned, understanding the behaviors of animal spirits simply involves common sense. I have owned and worked with animals myself for many, many years. When I was younger, I trained as a dog and cat groomer and later opened my own grooming shop. My husband and I also showed dogs for many years. From talking with animal communicators I have met, I have learned that most animals believe they are here for specific purposes. When they die, most animals will instinctively go into the white Light, knowing they have fulfilled their purpose on earth. Like humans, they may see familiar friends (both animal and human) in the Light and may be eager to join them.

But for some animals, training or loyalties may override their instincts, causing them to choose to remain earthbound. I once was called to a home to see if I could help the owner of a service dog figure out why her once-reliable companion had suddenly become inconsistent in his training. Buddy was a gorgeous black Lab who had been trained as a companion to a young woman named Carrie who suffered from seizures and other disorders. Carrie's first dog, Gilda, was a golden Lab who'd been with her for more than six years. As Gilda aged, she developed arthritis and poor vision and was no longer dependable as a service dog.

The trainer who had provided the family with Gilda suggested that Gilda stay with the family even after the new dog arrived. Carrie was thrilled with this arrangement. She didn't want to give up her beloved dog and even thought that Gilda might be able to teach the new pup a thing or two.

To everyone's relief, the two dogs got along famously. Gilda did seem to be teaching Buddy how to take over her job while relishing her new role of family pet. She loved to go for rides in the car and would still perform some of the simpler tasks, such as fetching items for her owner. Sadly, only ten months after her "retirement," Gilda became ill and died.

At first the family was willing to excuse Buddy's erratic behavior, saying that he was grieving for his companion. But after a while, everyone, including the trainer, was mystified by his refusal to perform certain commands he had been trained to do.

Finally Carrie's mother called me to ask if Gilda's ghost might somehow still be with them, confusing Buddy. I said I thought it was possible, and when I visited the home, I wasn't surprised when Gilda's ghost met me at the door with her tail wagging. Buddy trailed respectfully behind his mentor. "See," Carrie said as she let me in. "Buddy is supposed to get to the door either with or before me. Not *after* I answer it. He does stuff like this all the time."

The trainer had come to the house as well, and I asked her if it was common practice to put a newer dog with an older one for training. She said that she had done it with Seeing Eye dogs, but not as much with service dogs, which need to know how to perform multiple tasks. I suggested that maybe Gilda's ghost was confusing Buddy. I asked Carrie to give Buddy one of the commands he had become lax about performing.

"He's the worst at fetch," she told me. She told Buddy to go get the television remote. Gilda's ghost left the room first, with Buddy and me following closely behind her. Both dogs reached the remote, and then Gilda put her paw over it while poor Buddy simply sat and stared, as if trying to figure out how he was expected to retrieve the very item Gilda had claimed.

Once I explained to everyone what was happening, they all agreed that it would be best for Gilda to cross over. Because of her specialized training, I wasn't sure how I was going to get Gilda to go into the Light. It was going to be a matter of trial and error. At first I made the Light and pointed toward it. "Go see!" I told Gilda. But she just sat and stared at me impassively.

Realizing that Gilda was trained to take commands only from her owner and trainer, and that neither of them could see where I was making the Light, I knew I had to get creative. I told the trainer to get something that Gilda knew she was supposed to fetch, but to make sure it was something that wouldn't break. The trainer came back from her van with a disabled cell phone that she explained she often used for practice with the dogs. I pointed to where I planned to make the Light. Then I told the trainer to put the cell phone there and—when I gave her the signal—to send Gilda to retrieve it. I hoped that since Gilda's ghost hadn't been able to pick up the TV remote earlier, she'd be unable to do anything with the phone and would simply stay with it as I closed the Light behind her.

The plan worked better than I could have hoped, and I was

able to cross Gilda over. According to the family and the trainer, Buddy remained confused for a few days. Once he realized that he was again in charge, though, he resumed his duties and became a faithful and dependable service dog.

Of course, understanding that animal ghosts usually behave just as the living animal would didn't always offer me much peace of mind. Because of my history with dogs, I was pretty sure I would be able to deal with the earthbound spirits of most dogs, but as a cat owner, I dreaded the first time I'd have to get a cat into the Light.

When I finally did encounter the ghost of a cat—at a home where a kitten had begun to pick up some extremely submissive behaviors, even though she was the only animal in the house—I was fortunate that there was also a human ghost present. And although the lady hadn't been much of a cat person while she was alive, she grudgingly agreed to take the ghost cat into the Light with her—much to the relief of the terrorized kitten, who didn't seem sad at all to see her nemesis leave.

From that visit on, I've used this technique whenever I can; it's just the simplest way to get an animal to cross over. Fortunately, there are certain places where I'm pretty sure I'll encounter both animal and human spirits. For instance, fire stations are often in-habited by both the earthbound spirits of old firefighters and the ghosts of the dalmatians who were the stations' mascots. More than once, the ghost of a helpful firefighter has been pleased to take a loyal dog's spirit into the Light. And at racetracks, I've been able to find the ghosts of grooms who are willing to lead the earthbound spirits of fiery racehorses into the Light.

Why Animals Stay

I believe that many animals stay earthbound out of a sense of loyalty. Most of the animal spirits I have encountered have been with a human whom they loved, or in a home that was familiar to them. Other animal spirits, especially dogs, stay because they intend to comfort people. I know that my beloved bichon, Major, stayed with me after he died, although all my other show dogs crossed over.

Still other animals apparently linger to offer protection. When I do radio shows, I often get a lot of calls from long-distance truckers who are listening as they drive. Most of them have had an encounter with what I call "highway animals." These ghosts are usually white dogs, though I have heard of people who have seen bears or coyotes. The drivers explain that they were driving on a quiet stretch of highway when suddenly they saw a big white dog in the road, usually when they were cresting a hill or starting a deep curve. They slammed on the brakes to avoid hitting the animal and proceeded cautiously. Almost always, they then saw—slightly up ahead—a person standing by the side of the highway, or an accident, or a disabled vehicle. To these drivers, it was as if the animals were purposely warning them of a danger ahead.

I have also heard from people who do not have pets at home but have been startled awake at night by the sound of a dog frantically barking or the feeling of a cat batting at their face. Once awake, they become aware of some kind of emergency such as a fire or a seriously ill family member.

And I've seen animals stay out of a sense of a job unfinished. I have encountered ghost racehorses that still exercise themselves on the track each morning and run in actual races with the living horses. In the end, much like humans, I believe that animals' personalities influence whether their spirits stay behind or cross over.

Recognizing When an Animal Ghost Is Present

When I do visit someplace where a ghost animal is present, people frequently ask me, "Why didn't my dog/cat/canary sense this ghost?" Again, my experience has shown that animals are very like people in this regard. Animals notice both animal and human earthbound spirits and react to them as they would to any living animal or person in their space. They may also be more sensitive to the subtle changes in temperature that can occur around earthbound spirits.

Like some people, some animals are more aware of the presence of earthbound spirits in general. There are animals that will notice if a spirit comes into a home, but if they move with their family into a house where ghosts are already present, they act as if the spirit belongs with the home. In this situation, an animal will largely ignore the presence of the earthbound spirit unless the ghost torments the pet by poking or kicking it, slamming doors on its tail, stepping on its paws, or trapping it in certain rooms.

Depending on the type of animal you have in your home, you may notice different behavior patterns—the spirits of animals definitely influence the living animals. For example, your cat may be peacefully sleeping in a sunny spot on the back of the couch when, suddenly, she'll wake up and intently track something across the floor or even the ceiling. If you are in the room, you'll follow your cat's gaze, but you won't see anything. Maybe you'll tell yourself that she's just noticing a bug or a spider. But nine times out of ten, if you get up and go look at the spot where she was staring, you won't find anything there.

Both dogs and cats may avoid certain areas in a room. They may suddenly stop dead in their tracks and turn around or take a different route out of a room. But unless there is an animal or human ghost that is purposely mean or threatening to them, animals are pretty laid-back about the earthbound spirits they see.

Are Animal Ghosts Harmful?

Because the ghosts of domestic animals are small, they don't need the same amount of energy as human spirits. And generally, having the earthbound spirit of a house pet in your home will not disturb you very much. In many cases, people who say they can sense the presence of beloved pets who have died tell me that they feel comforted. However, an animal's earthbound spirit can upset the other animals in the house and cause some problems. It's hard to discipline a badly behaved pet that you can't see!

When we were showing dogs, I was friendly with a very successful handler named Barry. He showed a variety of breeds for many clients. He had a very busy kennel in the state where he lived; it wasn't unusual for him to board twenty or thirty of his clients' show dogs at any given time. I met him when I noticed him in the show ring with a magnificent harlequin Great Dane. The dog's name was Duke, and he loved Barry. The two had a bond that made them a spectacular pair in the show ring. Out of the ring, Duke was as clumsy as a puppy. Given his huge size, he never went anywhere without leaving a wake of chaos.

I hadn't seen Barry for a while when we went to a dog show near his home. He invited us to stay with him and kennel our dogs at his facility. Well, it was a long drive home, so we accepted his offer. I asked about Duke and was sad to hear that he had died a few months earlier. I hadn't seen Duke's ghost with Barry earlier at the show, so I assumed he had crossed over. As we headed down to the kennel to lock up the dogs for the night, Barry told me that he hoped that they'd stay in their cages until morning. When I asked him what he meant, he told me that lately he'd been finding the kennel area a mess when he came in to see the dogs early in the morning. Towels from the grooming table would be strewn across the floor, dog toys would be flung all over the place, kibble would be spilled, and many of the dogs would appear to be exhausted, as if they'd been up all night at some big party.

"The weird thing," he added, "is that when I leave at night, I double-check to ensure that all the kennel doors are closed securely. And when I come back in the morning, they're all still locked tight. But the place is trashed. I can't figure out who could be doing this."

I had a pretty good idea, but I didn't say anything until we walked into the kennel. There was no question about what I saw: Duke's ghost was standing at the grooming table, his front paws up on the edge. He was almost as tall as me, and his tail began wagging a million miles an hour when Barry walked in. I didn't have one doubt about how all those towels were ending up on the floor each night.

Barry didn't believe me at first when I told him that Duke was there. "It's impossible," he said. "He wasn't with me when he died."

I asked him when the problems in the kennel had started. About three weeks ago, he told me, ever since he had returned from a dog show several states away. I asked if he'd seen Duke's owners at that show; he had. They had brought one of Duke's puppies to have him assess the pup's show potential. "We were talking about how much the pup looked like Duke," he said. He stopped talking and stared at me for a long minute.

I just nodded. "He's really here," I said.

As much as Barry loved Duke, there was no way the dog's ghost could stay. Barry gave me one of Duke's old favorite toys and watched as I made the Light and threw the toy into it. Duke wagged his tail happily and bounded in after it.

As sad as Barry was to say good-bye to an old friend, there was no denying his relief the next morning when we came down to the kennel to find perfect order and peacefully snoozing dogs.

The presence of ghost animals can sometimes put both animals and humans at risk. Because my home is so close to Kentucky, I have done a lot of work at racetracks in that area and have seen many situations where the presence of ghost horses endangers both other horses and the people around them. Ghost racehorses that run on the track during regular races can distract the other horses, causing them to spook or swerve. After several spectacular on-course collisions, one standardbred racetrack (where the horses trot around pulling little buggy-like carts called sulkies) called and asked me to visit. While I was there, I was able to send several ghost horses and their drivers into the Light and make the track safer for the living horses competing on it.

My first experience with ghost horses came thanks to friends of ours who own and race Thoroughbreds. One day in conversation, my friend Edie mentioned that her horse Lola's Back in Town—Lola for short—had begun acting strange in her morning workouts. Edie asked if I would come to the track and watch the horse run.

Now, I had never been around horses much, and I certainly hadn't spent a lot of time at the track, but when I got to Chicago and went to the racetrack I was fascinated. Let me tell you, racetracks are just *loaded* with earthbound spirits. There are the ghosts of the grooms and trainers, many of whom practically grew up on the track. There are the ghosts of jockeys—both good ones and those who might charitably be called a bit shady—as well as the spirits of old gamblers and those they call rail birds, the fellows who hang out at the track all day watching the workouts, timing the horses, and honing their betting skills. And of course, there are ghost racehorses.

Given all the energy generated at probably any racetrack in the world, I can understand why they're so attractive to earthbound spirits. Nor am I surprised by how much energy some of these spirits have—enough to affect some of the daily events in the barns and on the track. On the other side of this equation, having all these earthbound spirits, human and equine, congregating in one area can result in some terrible problems. I expected to hear all kinds of hard-luck stories, and I wasn't disappointed. The jockeys shared endless tales of bad health and unexpected injuries, and the grooms pointed out areas in the barn and on the track where the horses were guaranteed to act up. I was also surprised to learn that as large as racehorses are, they are surprisingly delicate. They can be susceptible to respiratory conditions, and unfortunately, just as with humans, the presence of earthbound spirits can contribute to these conditions.

Although I didn't know exactly what I was supposed to be looking for when I went to watch Lola, I figured it out as soon as I saw the ghost horse and jockey join the others at the starting gate. Lola got off to a strong start, but it wasn't long before the ghost horse was pulling up alongside her. I saw the ghost jockey flick his whip, and Lola took a step to the side. It was a tiny movement, but it was enough for another horse in the pack to blast past her and win the race.

When I told my friend Edie and her husband, Ken, what I had seen, they confirmed my suspicions. Waving a whip at another horse during a race is a serious foul: Lola's step to the side could have bumped her into one of the live horses she was racing against. They asked me how we could solve the problem.

I had an idea, but it meant that we had to talk to Lola's trainer. Gabe was a handsome Irish fellow, and I assumed he might have some superstitions of his own. Nevertheless, when it came to convincing him that a ghost horse had caused his prized filly to lose her race, he was pretty dubious. It wasn't until I told him about the earthbound spirit of a jockey who was standing right outside his office that he began to take me seriously. I gave him the man's name and described how he had died: During a race, both horse and rider had fallen. The rider was killed, and the horse had to be humanely put down.

After that, Gabe agreed to let me try hanging a small charm containing a quince seed on all Lola's bridles. After she won her next two races, he invited me back to the barn. We put charms on all his horses' bridles, and then he asked me to clear his stalls and offices of any lingering spirits. I did my best, but I have to admit that my horsemanship skills might be a bit lacking. I was able to get a few of the ghost jockeys to jump up on the horses and ride them into the Light. Some of the ghost grooms walked ghost horses in on lead ropes. But one particular stallion would not go into the Light, and I could not convince any of the earthbound spirits to get near him. I suspect he's still out there running races.

9

EVIL SPIRITS

Rare but Real

THIS CHAPTER is brief, because frankly I don't like talking about evil spirits any more than I like having to encounter them. Thankfully, in all the years that I've been dealing with earthbound spirits, I haven't had to contend with very many of these dark and powerful negative forces. I want to be very clear that the entities I am talking about in this chapter are completely different from the earthbound spirits of normal people who have died. In some of the previous stories in this book, I talked about the earthbound spirits of people who acted in evil ways when they were alive. When these "bad" people—murderers, rapists, pedophiles, or other criminals—die, they are still welcomed into the Light. And when I encounter their earthbound spirits, I still offer them the chance to go into the white Light. As I've said before, I do not know what happens to these spirits after they enter the Light. What I do know, however, is that the Light is there for them at the time of death.

I also want to be very clear that when I talk about dark entities or evil spirits in this chapter, I am talking specifically about spirits that *are not of the Light*. These entities do not come from the Light. In fact, I do not believe that they were ever human. When

I encounter these spirits, I do make the Light—mostly for my own protection—but only rarely am I able to send the spirit into it. When I tell a dark spirit to leave, it generally *will* leave the person or the place where it has been attached, but I don't always know where it goes. I have come to believe that these dark entities basically recycle through the universe, moving from place to place or person to person as they are summoned or welcomed.

Although the evil spirits, or dark entities, that I am talking about here are energy forms, they are not the same as the negative energy I refer to throughout this book. Simple negative energy can take the form of a curse or of bad thoughts directed with intent at a specific person. Some earthbound spirits contribute to negative energy. Some living people do, too.

The evil spirits I address in this chapter, on the other hand, are specifically used in negative ways—for instance, to give people power when practicing dark arts such as certain forms of black magic or satanism. The people who summon these entities often do so expecting to be endowed with extraordinary powers. Those whom I have met and helped have admitted that they did not understand the full extent of the dangers they were exposing themselves and their loved ones to when they invited these dark entities into their lives.

How Dark Spirits Are Summoned

Any number of rituals can be used to summon spirits. While Ouija boards generally attract the attention of earthbound spirits, they can occasionally invite other entities into a home. I do get a fair number of calls from people who are afraid that they have evil spirits—often they tell me it's the devil—in their homes. In almost every case, they don't. These entities require a kind of energy that's simply not found in a normal home. The people who do have evil spirits in their presence have usually participated in rituals designed specifically to attract them. In a few extremely rare instances, I have worked with individuals who have been unfortunate enough to unknowingly move into a home where the previous occupants had practiced these dark rituals.

One young couple called me after they had moved into their new home. When the wife became pregnant with their first child and they began house-hunting, they had been excited to find the old Mission-style home in a quiet town on the U.S. side of the Mexican border. Unfortunately, their excitement turned to unease after they moved in and began renovating. The house had been empty for several years and needed a lot of cosmetic work. When they took down the wallpaper, they discovered pentagrams drawn on the walls. While working in a crawl space under the house, the husband found a mirror decorated with symbols he didn't recognize. There was an old Ouija board hung up on the wall inside one of the closets on the second floor.

They didn't think it was a coincidence that their move also marked the onset of a series of complications in the pregnancy. When I arrived at the house, I could immediately sense an incredible amount of negative energy. While I did not encounter any dark entities, I did have the sense that such evil forces had been in the home at one time.

I explained to the couple that the pentagrams on the wall might have been intended to serve as portals. Portals are energy openings between the mortal and spirit worlds that allow spirits to come and go at will. They are usually created in rituals involving specific symbols drawn on walls or floors. Those dabbling in black magic or black witchcraft often use the symbolism without fully comprehending the powers they are invoking. I have seen cases where, even in houses I have cleared of spirits and protected with quince seeds, a kid fooling around with dark witchcraft or black magic has blown open a portal and allowed spirits to return to the house. It is important to remember that, if spirits can come and go through portals, dark forces can use them as openings into your life as well.

I cleared the couple's home of the negative energy (using the techniques I explain in chapter 13) and put up quince seeds to offer protection. The husband dropped off the mirror and Ouija board at a church at the end of their street. Last I heard, the wife's pregnancy had stabilized, and the couple were enjoying their new home.

Possessions

When people invite dark spirits to enter their bodies, they become possessed—or controlled—by this evil force. Such possessions differ from other, more harmless types such as those that occur through "walk-ins." During a walk-in, a spirit takes advantage of an unconscious or near-dead person to inhabit or walk into the body. Walk-in ghosts are commonly found in the bodies of people who are diagnosed as having come back to life after being declared dead. For instance, imagine that a man has gone to a public park to commit suicide. He overdoses on pills and is near death when passersby spot him, unconscious, and call for help. On arrival, paramedics cannot find a pulse, but they work to resuscitate him anyway. In the meantime, a passing spirit takes advantage of the situation to enter the empty shell of a body and take up residence. The paramedics are suddenly shocked to discover a weak pulse. The man is "saved" from death. But in fact, what has survived is very different from the man who died, although in ways that are distinctly mundane. Perhaps the man who attempted to take his life had always hated classical music. After his revival, those who know him are shocked to find that he now adores Mozart. Or a person who formerly loved dogs will suddenly acquire two cats. Perhaps someone who hated spicy foods will crave Mexican dishes. These new traits are definitely changes, and can be very disturbing to friends and relatives who wonder what has happened to their loved one. Still, for the most part they're harmless.

Possessions by dark entities are nowhere near as innocent. People who have allowed an evil spirit to take up residence in their bodies often hear voices. They may behave bizarrely but have no recollection of their actions. Those suffering from possession share many characteristics with people who are mentally ill, and they may be hospitalized for treatment of a mental disorder. There is no way for a layperson to distinguish between the force of these dark energies and the very real problems of mental or chemical imbalances. Many churches and religions, however, recognize the threat of spirit possessions, and most have specialized members to deal with them who can offer guidance to those worried they may have encountered dark spirits.

In my years of helping earthbound spirits cross over, I have met all kinds of ghosts, but only a very few people who were possessed by a truly evil entity. In a handful of cases, I have worked with people to remove dark energy using some of the techniques my grandmother taught me for removing curses. This kind of work, however, is much more dangerous and difficult than removing a curse or negative energy. I have been both deeply uncomfortable and physically harmed the few times I have confronted these dark entities. I absolutely do not seek out this kind of work: I prefer to leave it to others who are trained and knowledgeable in dealing with these forces.

The Power of Dark Entities

Dark entities, evil spirits, demons—whatever names they are given—have a lot of power. These are the forces that can move heavy pieces of furniture, tip over bookshelves, and kill or seriously injure pets or small animals. Some folks have told me about glimpsing shadowy black forms drifting through their homes. Others mention the unnerving appearance of blood-red eyes that seem to float in darkness. Still other people have told me of spotting creatures with hooves, horns, or tails, though I myself have never seen any earthbound spirit with these characteristics.

It is worth repeating that these entities seek out extremely negative energy. They are not commonly found in households. Usually they are summoned to be present through dangerous practices and are drawn to negative acts. And when they are present, they are unmistakable.

I visited one house after a woman called me to say she had been frightened by glimpsing red eyes in the darkness of one of her rooms. When I pulled up to the curb, even before I had stepped out of my car I could tell that the energy around the house was not good. I had prepared to encounter something nasty, but still felt uneasy as I moved from room to room watching as the shades or blinds in each window suddenly unrolled. Each room was plunged into darkness as I entered it. I asked the woman if this happened often; she told me with a sigh that she spent most of her day moving from room to room, opening drapes and raising shades, only to have the room sink back into gloom before she even got to the doorway.

I did clear some dark energy from that home. And as always when I work with malevolent spirits, I learned nothing about them. These entities never speak to me. I have tried to communicate with them. I have asked them for their names, the reasons for their deaths, and where their bodies are buried, but I have never received an answer from these dark, human-like forms—just menacing glares.

I've come to believe that these entities are not like earthbound spirits, and that I may never be able to communicate with them. Because of my experience in removing curses and other negative energies, I do believe I can send these types of dark entities away from a person or a place. But I will admit that I don't know where they go when they leave.

Protecting Yourself from Evil Spirits

The best way to protect yourself from dark energy is to prevent such entities from being attracted to you in the first place. Do not dabble in black arts, dark witchcraft, or satanism. Do not play with Ouija boards of any type. Do not perform spells intended to summon a spirit to grant you greater power or wealth or fame.

Some of the techniques I recommend later on in this book for dealing with curses and other negative energies may help weaken the influence of a dark entity that has become attached to you or your home. If you continue to suffer, seek out counseling from a trusted spiritual or religious adviser.

Most important, remember that almost all the ghosts I deal with are the earthbound spirits of distinct individuals. These ghosts behave just as they did when they were alive. They can be annoying, their need for energy can cause problems for you and your family, and they may even be unpleasant. But the evil spirits I have discussed in this chapter do not behave like humans. In my experience, they are darker, less predictable, and more dangerous than even the most intimidating ghost I have ever met.

PART III

Living with Ghosts

10

ASKING FOR TROUBLE

How People Attract Earthbound Spirits

ONE OF the first questions I hear when I clear a ghost from someone's home is: "Is it the ghost of my mother/father/close relative?" It might surprise you to learn that most of the time, the answer is no. While some earthbound spirits initially seek out their close family members, after a while they seem to realize that the physical ailments and other troubles plaguing their spouses or children are directly related to their ghostly presence. And although I have encountered a few ghosts who seem to take delight in making their families miserable, most earthbound spirits do not wish to cause problems for the loved ones they've left behind.

After I pass along what I've learned from speaking with a particular earthbound spirit—name and age, manner of death, place of burial—many people go on to find out more about that spirit's life. In some of these situations, it has turned out that the people did casually know the person who died, or were able to recollect how they might have come into contact.

Nevertheless, in many, many of the houses I visit, living and dead remain strangers to each other. "Well, what's *he* doing here?" a puzzled homeowner will ask when I tell her about the ghost of the middle-aged man in her basement who keeps short-circuiting the wiring in her furnace. I can understand her bewilderment completely. How *do* people end up sharing their homes with ghostly strangers?

I Was Here First

Sometimes people move into houses or apartments that are already inhabited. If a home is empty for only a short while, resident ghosts won't necessarily leave to seek a new source of energy. Particular earthbound spirits are very attached to a specific place for any number of reasons. As long as they are able to find a source of energy, they may choose to return to an empty home and await the next owner.

If you have recently bought a home and are in the midst of renovations prior to moving in, pay attention to your contractors when they tell you how the work is going. Unexplained delays, unexpected accidents, and an air of tension surrounding the project could be the work of energy-starved ghosts. Renovations can also irritate homebody ghosts, who may become angry at changes being made to what they consider "their" home.

One couple called me after having moved into their dream house. They'd spent months searching for the perfect home and were sure that their eight-year-old twin sons would love it, too. The plan had been for each boy to have his own room, but the pair soon refused to sleep apart. So their parents decided to use the spare room as a temporary playroom while the basement playroom was remodeled. From the beginning, the renovations in the basement were fraught with problems. As soon as the father started the work, everything seemed to go wrong—from misplaced screwdrivers to badly cut lumber and minor injuries. Worse, he felt stifled and extremely irritable whenever he went into the basement. For no apparent reason, the unpleasant feelings seemed to last for hours after he finished his work. Finally, the new playroom was completed, and the boys decided that they wanted their own rooms after all. For about two weeks, everything was perfect. But soon, the twins' mother started finding the boys asleep in the same bed, and they resisted playing in their beautiful new playroom in the basement.

One day, their mother overheard the boys talking at the bottom of the basement stairs. Their voices sounded frightened and confused.

"I don't know why she makes us come down here with that guy," one said.

"She doesn't know about him, dummy," the other quipped, then added solemnly, "He scares me."

"Yeah, it's really freaky the way he just stands and stares at us."

"And he breaks my toys!"

Their mother didn't know what to make of the conversation, but it wasn't long before she, too, began noticing odd occurrences in the basement. Their newly installed washer and dryer broke repeatedly. Then the bathroom began requiring repairs. She dismissed these incidents and the boys' comments until the day when the situation took a more serious turn.

The mother was heading down the basement stairs carrying a load of laundry when the two boys came racing up the stairs toward her, clearly terrified. They stopped midway, and one boy turned and fixed his attention on a point in the air just in front of his mother. Frightened, he stumbled on the stairs and fell backward, accidentally taking his brother with him.

"Oh my God!" their mother cried, rushing down to the bottom of the stairs where the boys had landed. They were both extremely shaken, but fortunately unharmed.

"What happened?" asked their mother, alarmed.

"We keep telling you!" cried the twin who had stumbled, his eyes welling with tears. "It's that man! He was down here again! We were coming to get you when he suddenly appeared on the steps, right in front of you."

"He growled at us," the other one piped in timidly. "He's scary."

The mother felt the hair on her neck stand up, and she glanced around at the basement. Despite the bright colors and veritable wonderland of toys, the room did feel sinister in a subtle way. It was something she'd noticed before but never really consciously thought about. She recalled her husband's experiences during the renovation: his accidents, his bad moods.

When she called me, I knew right away that there was something negative in the house. Not an evil entity, but definitely the ghost of a negative person. And that's exactly what I found when I visited their home: an angry older man who disliked children. He had once lived in the house and was extremely unhappy when the basement—*his* basement—was turned into a playroom. The ghost of this older gentleman was pleasant when I spoke with him and quite happy to cross over when I gave him the option. With peace restored, the family could finally settle into their dream home.

Earthbound spirits often seem particularly reluctant to leave theaters. At any given time, most theaters are filled with earthbound spirits. Of course, this makes perfect sense. Not only is there a constant flow of energy—from stagehands and mechanics working on the sets to actors rehearsing scenes to theatergoers lost in the drama playing out before them—but many theater ghosts are acting wannabes or starstruck fans or directors, designers, or other behind-the-scenes professionals with control issues. When I began working on *Ghost Whisperer*, I discovered that the same holds true for soundstages and Hollywood lots. Not surprisingly, the film industry attracts earthbound spirits for the same reasons as the theatrical business.

In my experience, earthbound spirits who are attached to places rather than individuals are mostly quite willing to cross over when I offer them the option. Because they do not have any specific unfinished business or need to communicate with the living, I can usually persuade them to move on to somewhere that is better for them.

You Took My Things

Ghosts can end up in your home when you bring in an object that was once theirs. Whether you inherit your great-aunt's silver or are a flea-market enthusiast, the more secondhand, antique, or hand-me-down items you have in your home, the greater your chances of collecting a few ghosts as well.

I am still amazed by the objects that can exert such powerful holds. Some seem more obvious than others. I'd estimate that about 75 percent of all estate jewelry comes with a ghost attached. Many women stay to look after their favorite diamonds; men worry about their expensive watches and are very attached to their cars. I've come across ghosts who have stayed to keep track of mink coats, bedroom sets, or wedding gowns. I've even encountered a few who were so sentimental about a set of dishes or a treasured shaving mug that they refused to cross over until they knew what would happen to it.

I did some work for a woman I'd first met when her husband suddenly died, leaving her a young widow with two small children. She had asked me to come to the funeral, and I was able to help her by sharing some important information about the family's finances from her husband.

Many years later, I got another call from her when renovations on her home revealed a shocking surprise. This woman, it turns out, was an avid flea-market shopper. She collected vintage silverware and other small silver items like baby mugs and hairbrush and mirror sets. She couldn't go to a tag sale, flea market, or estate sale without picking up a few more sterling spoons, forks, or knives. She used to joke with me that she had to collect so many of each item because she was always misplacing her silverware.

When her children grew up and moved out of their two-bedroom home she decided to completely renovate it—she wanted it to be comfortable and practical for her as she aged. When the contractors began to take down the ceiling in the kitchen, they were pelted with a torrent of silverware! All the missing forks, knives, and spoons came raining out of the ceiling. There must have been fifty or sixty pieces.

When I arrived, I met the very crabby ghost of a man who was quite peeved that we had discovered his secret stash. He'd been a butler for a posh family and had been outraged when the children had decided to sell off their parents' silver. He had followed the woman home from an estate auction and for the last ten years had taken great delight in hiding a few pieces of silver from every collection she purchased. He admitted that it hadn't been as much fun in later years, when the woman finally decided that it was perfectly acceptable to mix and match silver patterns when setting her table, thus becoming less concerned if pieces suddenly went missing.

Moving all that silverware must have required a tremendous amount of energy, and after the children moved out, I believe it became increasingly difficult for him to carry on with his petty thievery. Once he was discovered, he admitted that he was indeed a bit weary of the whole thing and crossed over without any fuss at all.

If you are a flea-market fan or a tag-sale shopper or someone who has furnished your house with high-end antiques from estate sales, it is likely you are hosting an earthbound spirit or two as well. You don't have to stop bargain shopping, however. In chapter 12, I'll give you tips for helping to protect your purchases from any earthbound spirits who may be intent on coming home with them.

I Was Invited

When I'm asked to clear out spirits and the ghosts tell me they were basically invited in, I have to admit that I do become frustrated. The thing is, I receive literally thousands of requests for help each month. Many people contact me on the basis of my reputation—whether they've heard of me from friends or family, or heard me speak on a radio show, or attended one of my lectures or workshops—and they are the ones who usually have strong intuitions about being in the presence of an earthbound spirit.

Other people don't have a personal reference when they call or write or contact me through my Web site. These folks are often worried; some are frantic, and a few I'd characterize as desperate. They're reaching out to me because they are experiencing serious problems with their health, their homes, or their families and, having exhausted all the logical explanations for the troubles they are dealing with, are calling me as a last resort. Many are so anxious for me to visit their homes that they call again and again, ignoring the message on my answering machine that says it can take me up to four months to return their calls.

And more often than not, when I finally do arrive at their homes, I encounter earthbound spirits with attitude problems. When they learn that I can see and communicate with them, they wonder why I am there at all. After all, these ghosts tell me, they are attached to the person or home only because they were invited to stay. When I question the people who called me, I often find out that, yes, they were recently using a Ouija board/had a séance/tried a dark witchcraft ritual/attempted to cast a spell.

I try not to get upset with these folks—at least not the first time I'm called to their house. Most people don't fully understand the powers of such acts. But the simple fact is this: While some earthbound spirits attach to people who are innocent bystanders, so to speak, others are drawn by the energies that surround meta-physical objects or acts used incorrectly.

What I wish people would understand is that they can easily attract ghosts—and all the problems associated with ghosts—by messing around with metaphysical objects such as Ouija boards, pendulums, or tarot cards. Attempting to practice dark witchcraft or cast spells can draw ghosts. Hosting a séance invites spirits right into your home. Ghosts can be drawn to you if you attempt to enter meditative states for the purpose of communing with spirits. Automatic writing—in which you invite a spirit to move your hand to gain certain information via what you write—is particularly foolish, because it invites spirits into your body and could lead to a possession.

There is absolutely no reason for average people to attempt these methods of contacting spirits. If any spirits urgently need to communicate with you, they will find a way. Spirits who have gone into the Light can communicate via dreams. And if there are earthbound spirits that absolutely need to get your attention, you can believe me that they come up with a way to get it. There is no good reason to choose to share your environment with an earthbound spirit.

I have had people tell me that they invited a spirit into their home to gain some greater psychic connection and higher knowledge of the spirit world. I want to assure you that the spirits who are attracted to people through these methods are almost always earthbound spirits. And because earthbound spirits have not gone into the Light, they don't know anything more about the lives and powers of the spirit world than they did when they were alive.

I Followed You Home

Even if you haven't been playing with a Ouija board or dabbling in dark witchcraft, it's quite possible that you come into contact with earthbound spirits on a regular basis. And it's further likely that, eventually, you will bring someone home with you. The bottom line is, if you have a high-energy, Type A personality; if you have very high levels of physical energy—if you're a professional athlete or performer, for instance—or if you work outside the home, especially in a job where you interact with the public, it's likely only a matter of time until you attract a ghost. Earthbound spirits need energy, so wherever there are people in energized situations, there are ghosts.

Over the years, I've noticed that certain kinds of jobs tend to attract ghosts. This list is constantly evolving as I continue to visit new places and add to my own understanding about where earthbound spirits congregate. When I went to California, it made sense to me that I'd encounter ghosts on TV or movie sets. However, my stay in Santa Monica was also the first time I had seen groups of homeless people living on the streets. I suspected that there would be a lot of earthbound spirits hanging around them, but the opposite was true: There were almost no spirits around the homeless. Although I can predict what kinds of situations will most likely attract earthbound spirits, until I have had the opportunity to actually spend time in one, I just don't know for sure.

Here, then, is my list of the places and professions where earthbound spirits are most likely to be found:

- **Emergency rooms,** especially in city hospitals. Doctors, nurses, and ambulance attendants are particularly vulnerable to attracting ghosts, although simply sitting in the waiting room can be enough to get you noticed by an earthbound spirit.
- **Nursing homes.** These spots are particularly crowded with the ghosts of elderly men, probably waiting for their wives to pass. I don't often see the ghosts of women waiting around for their husbands.
- **Bars.** The rowdier, the better. Earthbound spirits can thrive on the energy generated in a typical biker bar or "punch palace," where smashed glasses and overturned tables are barely reason to look up from your drink. Just as in life, the establishment you frequent dictates the type of spirit you may attract. Ghosts passing time in hotel cocktail lounges are usually very different from those hanging out in topless bars.
- **Dental offices.** How many times have you sat frozen with tension and fear in the waiting room, listening for the hygienist to call your name? Does your dentist's office suffer from computer or electronic malfunctions? Lost appoint-

ments? How many times have you left vowing to find another dentist—or wondering why sitting in that chair freaks you out so much? The energy generated in these busy offices is intense.

- **Police stations.** It's rare that I've ever met a police officer who *didn't* have a spirit attached. These ghosts often have some unfinished business, usually having to do with how they ended up dead. The officer need not have been directly involved with the ghost's particular case.

- **Fire stations.** For reasons I have never understood, there are always plenty of earthbound spirits at fire stations, but they rarely go home with the firefighters.

- **Law offices or courtrooms.** Lawyers and judges who specialize in criminal cases run a higher risk of attracting earthbound spirits.

- **Mental health institutions.** People who are institutionalized often have earthbound spirits attached to them. Such ghosts may travel home with the staff as well.

- **Airports.** Airline personnel, flight attendants, and pilots all have a tendency to attract earthbound spirits from all over the world. If you spend a lot of time traveling or in airports, you may bring a ghost home from your travels.

- **Sports arenas.** There's no energy like the energy generated by rabid sports fans. I have worked with many professional athletes, who as a group tend to attract both spirits and negative energy in the course of their careers.

- **Publishing houses.** A year ago, I would not have expected to find earthbound spirits in publishing offices. Until I began writing this book, I had envisioned the book industry as a quiet, tranquil enterprise. And then I visited several publishing houses. Of course, once I saw the levels of activity and the floors and floors of high-energy individuals involved in book publishing, it made sense that so many ghosts could be found in these offices.

- **Antiques dealers.** Since many earthbound spirits like to stay with their treasured possessions, antiques and second-hand shops are usually home to several ghosts at any given time.

- **Theaters and movie sets.** In my lectures and on radio, I've often talked about how many earthbound spirits tend to gravitate to theaters, but I had never worked on a film lot before I became involved with *Ghost Whisperer*. Now I know that television and movie sets are full of ghosts. From my very first visit to the studio, I've had plenty of work to do convincing earthbound spirits that they're no longer needed on set. And believe me, given the personalities involved, this is not an easy task.

I met my first real, honest-to-goodness Hollywood star the first time I was on the Paramount lot. As is my habit, I was walking around the set, pad and pencil at the ready, prepared to take notes on any spirits I saw. And, as usual, there was a small crowd following me. We rounded a corner—and there she was. I stopped dead in my tracks and blurted out, "Oh my gosh, you're Miss Barbara Stanwyck!"

Some of the younger folk in the group were puzzled. "Who?"

"You know, Victoria Barkley, from *The Big Valley*," I said, hoping that the well-known TV show might give them some context. I was also hoping that if it didn't, they would just keep quiet. I could tell that Miss Stanwyck was none too pleased at their ignorance.

"Ah, some old TV actress," someone muttered, clearly losing interest.

Well, that did it. Miss Stanwyck was furious!

I quickly set the record straight, giving everyone present a brief education in just who Barbara Stanwyck was. How she had been a star of stage and screen—a pioneer in the industry. I mentioned her good looks, her talent, her work ethic, and her success.

"She's the real deal," I told everyone. "And you all need to show some respect."

When I finished my little speech, everyone was silent, and Barbara Stanwyck was looking mollified. Then, like any fan, I told her how much I admired her work. We talked for a long time. She was more than happy to chat with me about the various movies she'd been in. She told me that, while she was alive, she'd always believed in ghosts, and she'd been pleased to find out that she could stick around the industry that had been so important to her.

When we'd finished talking, I asked her if she wanted to go into the Light. To be honest, I was feeling a bit protective toward her. She'd been eighty-three when she died, and though she was still lovely, with high cheekbones and regal posture, she was also a tiny, frail-looking elderly woman. I thought that after years of hanging around, she'd be ready to leave.

"I don't think so," she replied politely but firmly. "I think I need to keep an eye on things around here."

From her answer, I knew that I absolutely couldn't patronize her. I was going to have to come up with a pretty good argument.

"Miss Stanwyck," I said respectfully, "don't you miss having your fans recognize you?"

She made a dismissive gesture with her hand, but I could tell I was on the right track.

"I imagine that I'm the first person who's seen you in a long time," I continued. "Has anyone else been able to speak to you?"

She shook her head.

"In the Light, you'll go back to your prime years," I said. "And spirits from the other side can choose to cross back and forth. You don't have that option right now."

She eyed me skeptically, but I could tell I was gaining ground, so I kept going. "Since I can see you and talk to you, don't you think I might know what I'm talking about?"

"I'll still be able to visit?" she asked.

"I have friends who communicate with spirits from the other side all the time," I reassured her. "I won't be able to see you or talk to you once you've gone into the Light, but there are others who will."

Her chin went up, and I could tell she'd made up her mind. "Fine," she said. "I'll go."

I made the Light and watched her walk into it. I actually felt pretty good about it. I do believe that spirits who cross over are at greater peace than those who remain earthbound. I'm happy to be able to give them the opportunity to change their circumstances.

My most recent visits to the set of *Ghost Whisperer* have revealed to me something I never imagined might happen: Earthbound spirits from other sets on the studio lots are gravitating to our set because of the subject matter. These earthbound spirits are attaching themselves to crew and cast, and especially to the actors who play the lead characters. After talking to some of these ghosts, I've come to realize that they, just like some real-life fans, have a hard time understanding that Jennifer Love Hewitt is not able to communicate with ghosts the way her character, Melinda, can. They have heard that there is someone on the set who can see and talk to earthbound spirits, so they go home with her and with other cast and crew members, hoping to attract notice. When they realize that the people they've followed home can't see them after all, the ghosts return to the set with them, only to cause more problems. Ultimately, these actors and crew members call me. I have to admit that this development, while disruptive to the show, has been effective—at least from the earthbound spirits' points of view. Each time I go out to Los Angeles to visit the set, I am able to release several ghosts into the Light, including a few rather well-known personalities. What I'm currently trying to figure out is how to protect the set from the unwanted effects of earthbound spirits. If you've ever seen film lots, you know how wide open they are. It's like trying to figure out how to protect a small city! If you are a visitor to theaters or TV or film sets, you may bring a spirit or two home with you when they decide they need a break from the performing arts.

As a person who works with the paranormal on a daily basis, I am always very aware of the energy around me. There are many other people who work in metaphysical fields—including card readers, astrologists, numerologists, spiritualists, healers, and more—and I urge them to be very cautious about protecting themselves during interactions with clients. Most people seek out the help of practitioners of these arts because they have something negative going on in their lives. If you are not taking proper precautions, such as keeping yourself in the white Light during the work, cleansing your equipment with sea salt and/or the energy of the moon, using protective talismans, and limiting your exposure to clients with profoundly negative energy, that negative energy—or any spiritual entities coming in the door with your clients—may stay around after the clients have departed. They may make your life more difficult, or they may attach to the next person who comes to you for help or advice. Because of your high likelihood of exposure to all kinds of spiritual entities, you must take extra care to protect yourself from their influences.

I also caution anyone who visits one of these practitioners to exercise care. If you are seeking an adviser in any of these areas, I always suggest that you get a recommendation from someone who has had work done by the person and has been satisfied. People who dabble in these arts without full knowledge can attract all kinds of negative energies or entities. There is no guarantee that after you visit your neighborhood card reader or storefront psychic, the ghost who was hanging around his or her office won't decide to go home with you.

It should be obvious after reading this chapter that there are all sorts of ways in which you may intentionally or unintentionally attract an earthbound spirit in the course of your daily routine. In chapter 11, I will discuss the signs that indicate that you may have attracted an earthbound spirit. In chapters 12 and 13, I give you specific steps for protecting yourself and your environment against earthbound spirits and negative energies, and tell you how to diminish the negative effects of unseen forces.

11

SIGNS THAT YOU ARE
NOT ALONE

Identifying the Presence of Spirits Around You

ONCE PEOPLE become aware of how easy it can be to attract ghosts and how often we share our environments with earthbound spirits, they naturally want to know how they can determine if they are in the presence of ghostly entities. Of course, it's easy for me to know for sure if there are earthbound spirits in your house: I can see them and clearly sense their energy. But there are many subtle and not-so-subtle signs that anyone can look for.

Remember that earthbound spirits need energy. They don't eat or sleep, but instead absorb emotional or physical energy generated by the living. Ghosts will do anything they can to cause reactions in the living people around them. The more energy ghosts have, the more dramatic their actions can be. Ghosts also draw energy from the full and new moons; during these times you may notice an increase in some of the phenomena discussed below.

If three or more of the signs below apply to you or your household and you don't have a good explanation for any of them, chances are you are living with an earthbound spirit.

Intuition

The first reaction I usually get after confirming for people that they do, indeed, have a ghost present is one of relief. "Oh, I just *knew* something was going on," they will say to me. The most important thing you can do to sense the presence of earthbound spirits is learn to trust your instincts. Most people want to be rational. They want to look for a simple explanation that will answer the questions lingering in their minds. But the spirit world is a complex world. Often people do not call me until they have exhausted all reasonable explanations for the odd events they are experiencing.

It is common for people who are living with earthbound spirits to have a sense that they are being watched. They feel uneasy when spending time in certain areas of their home. There's a good reason so many attics and basements feel "spooky" to people: These are two areas of the house where ghosts are frequently found.

You should be aware that both children and animals are usually quite sensitive to the more subtle disturbances that ghosts can cause. They will instinctively avoid areas where ghosts spend time. Your dog may refuse to accompany you down to your basement laundry area; your child may tell you the third-floor playroom feels "scary."

When you accept your own intuitive thoughts, you enhance your sensitivity to the presence of spirit energy. My husband, Ted, does not have the ability to see or talk to spirits—earthbound or otherwise. Granted, he's had more exposure over the years to ghosts than most people ever will. As a result, he's learned to keep an open mind and trust his instinct when he feels that a spirit might be present. For quite a few years, he worked at an auto dealership. And sometimes he'd get a used car into the dealership and experience a strong feeling that "something" was attached to it. He'd tuck these cars away at the back of the lot and give me a call. If I happened to be available that day, I'd swing by and check things out. Without fail, I'd find an earthbound spirit attached to the vehicle. Ted was right every time—and without using any special powers.

If, after checking out every rational explanation and reasonable theory as to why certain things are happening—in your home, with your health, or to your family, and particularly if you are experiencing any of the events I talk about below—you remain convinced that something is simply "off," trust your instincts. In chapter 12, I offer advice on diminishing the effects of earthbound spirits. Following some or all of these steps will do no harm and may, in fact, give you back the peace of mind that earthbound spirits can so easily disrupt.

Physical and Mental

Certain physical and mental symptoms are strongly associated with the presence of earthbound spirits.

Because all these symptoms are very common—and generally benign—you need to pay close attention to whether they're linked to any particular place (home, work, your car); whether you feel better once you leave that place; and if they occur on a regular basis. Identifying a pattern can help you determine the source of these troubles, whether it's as commonplace as a food allergy or slightly more exotic—like an earthbound spirit. I always recommend that people taking prescribed medications see their doctor once I have removed any ghosts or negative energy from their home or person. Often they are able to adjust their dose favorably once the negative energy has been cleared.

If you consistently suffer from any of the recurring symptoms below and doctors have repeatedly told you that they cannot find a medical reason for your nagging problems, you may want to consider whether you are suffering from exposure to an earthbound spirit.

Headaches

Headaches can also be a sign of a curse or negative energy. Pay particular attention to headaches that consistently affect you when you have spent time in one particular place.

A CPA once called me during tax season because she was suffering from debilitating headaches. I didn't really think it unusual for a tax preparer to get headaches. But when I listened closely to her message, I understood her concern. She would be fine all day at work—even though she was putting in fourteen-hour days. Then she'd go home and prepare to unwind with a glass of wine and some soft music. Instead of feeling a release from the day's pressures, though, she'd be hit with a blinding headache. She'd tried everything she could think of to ward off these headaches. She quit drinking red wine and switched to white. No relief. She quit drinking wine altogether. The headaches continued. She shut off the music. She went to her doctor. The doctor told her she wasn't suffering from migraines. He was puzzled as well. If she was suffering from tension headaches, they should occur at work.

It was a seemingly unconnected event that finally made her wonder if there could be an earthbound spirit in her house. One day she arrived home early and ran into her cleaning lady. The woman handed her a huge pile of mail—letters, bills, circulars, and magazines—and explained that she had found them stashed under the buffet in the dining room. She frequently found mail in that spot, she continued, and always left it on the dining room table before she left the house. The homeowner was puzzled: She'd *never* come home to find mail on the dining room table. Nevertheless, she assured her cleaner that she wasn't crazily hoarding mail under the buffet table (although at this point she was privately worrying if maybe the headaches were a symptom of her impending insanity).

Obviously she was very relieved to discover where all her bills had been going. As an accountant, she hated to miss payments or be late paying a bill. While she was trying to figure out how her mail had been hijacked, she mentioned the mystery of the mail to one of her tax clients who knew me. One thing led to another, and I received the call. Sure enough, when I went to her house there was a ghost living there as well. I released him into the Light. Since then, no more headaches and no more stress from missing mail!

Intestinal Problems

Lingering symptoms of discomfort, cramps, or vaguely queasy stomachs are common. Okay, I'll admit that these can be serious problems, but there was one instance that really gave me the giggles. The guy who called me was a real "gym Casanova" —you might recognize the type if you go to a health club. A muscle-bound fellow with a healthy ego, he loved to strut around the gym and hit on whatever attractive woman caught his attention. This guy was such a stereotype. When I went to his apartment, I almost laughed out loud. He lived in a total bachelor pad, complete with a circular bed made up with satin sheets.

A woman ghost who hung around at the gym had been attracted to him and had followed him home. Every time lover boy would bring home one of his conquests from the gym, he was suddenly struck with a case of nerves. He'd feel as if someone was watching him make his moves. Suddenly his great pickup didn't seem like such a good idea. Unfortunately for this Don Juan, his nerves manifested themselves as a terrible case of gas, followed by an incurable case of stomach upset. Word got around, and it became quite the joke at the gym. Although I did send the ghost into the Light, I'll admit that for one teeny-tiny second, I actually thought I'd be doing the women at the gym a big favor if I just let her stay with him.

Trouble Sleeping

Frequent waking in the night, difficulty falling asleep, and insomnia can all be signs of an earthbound spirit in your home.

Fatigue, Even When You Should Feel Rested

If your muscles constantly ache or feel heavy, if you have trouble waking up even after a good night's sleep, or if you feel you just aren't functioning at your best, your doctor may suggest that you are suffering from a chronic condition such as a thyroid disorder, anemia, or fibromyalgia. You might also consider this: The more energy a ghost absorbs, the less you have.

Unexplained Anxiety

Worrying over small matters, stressing out when you misplace things, or constantly assuming the worst in a harmless situation can all be signs of an earthbound spirit's influence.

Inappropriate Anger or Irritation

I have worked with plenty of couples on the brink of divorce and discovered that a ghost was the catalyst for their screaming fights—which trigger, at least for the ghost, a satisfying amount of emotional energy. Again, for an earthbound spirit it is easiest to manipulate the environment in ways that provoke stress responses. Leaving doors open, tossing underwear on the floor instead of in the hamper, accusing someone of misplacing the checkbook or of taking the car keys—all these common quarrels, when repeated again and again, can erode a relationship and damage the peace of a household.

Frequent Respiratory Infections; Colds; Ear or Throat Problems; Asthma

These symptoms are particularly common in children under the age of ten. Adults may also experience frequent sinus infections in addition to any of the other symptoms.

Vision Problems

You may have trouble focusing on certain objects in your home. For instance, a painting at the top of a stairway may not be plainly visible from the bottom of the stairs. You may have trouble seeing a television or computer monitor clearly, and no amount of adjustment can make the picture any sharper. People have told me they have seen flickers of light, moving shadows, or small patches of fog or mist drifting in a room. Sometimes people think they catch a glimpse of a human form or a bright light that looks like a person. Others mention seeing a shimmer in midair, like the disturbance created over asphalt on a hot summer's day.

Hearing

People living with earthbound spirits often think they hear someone saying their name. This may sound as if someone is calling them from far away—or as if someone's whispering right into their ear. In most but not all cases, this occurs while the people are sleeping, either at night in the moments just as they are dozing off or, more frequently, in the morning just before they awaken. Instead of being roused by the alarm clock, they will startle awake with their hearts pounding and adrenaline high, prepared to spring out of bed as they listen for another cry. Within a few minutes, it becomes clear that no one cried out; the room and house are peaceful and quiet. While most people dismiss these voices as coming from their dreams, there are others who cannot shake the feeling that someone called their name specifically to awaken them.

Other common phenomena include hearing footsteps in empty hallways or overhead, and hearing banging or pounding on doors or walls. I once did some work for a woman who wanted me to come while her husband wasn't at home. She didn't feel she could admit to him that she thought there were ghosts in the house. She was right, though: She had several ghosts of younger kids in her house, so I released them all into the Light and put up the protective quince seeds. As I was heading out the door, one of her older children asked what they should do when the teenage boy ghost came back. I told them that he wouldn't be able to enter the house, and that might make him angry for a few nights, but eventually he'd give up and go away.

A few days later, the woman took her kids to visit their grandparents for several nights. The husband was in the house alone. Of course, that was the night the teenage ghost decided to come back "home." Apparently, he spent the night in quite a huff, running around the house and banging on doors and windows, ringing the doorbell, and setting off the outdoor motion-detector lights. After a second night of this kind of noise, the husband called the police. The cops cruised by the house several times a night, but they never saw the neighborhood hooligans the husband was sure were tormenting him.

Each morning, the poor guy would start his day exhausted from the nightly racket. Finally, he couldn't take it. He called his wife and told her he was worried that he was having serious problems with his hearing—or maybe going crazy. He told her the whole story of the banging on the house.

Guiltily the wife confessed that I had been over to the house and had warned that such a thing might happen. At his wit's end and willing to try anything to get a good night's sleep, the husband called me. I spent part of the night sitting in their garage hoping that the ghost would show up. At 12:30 AM he finally arrived and started up with his noisy routine. I'll admit I got some satisfaction from the look on his face when I emerged from the garage and told him to knock it off. Once I sent him into the Light, it was the end of the banging and doorbell ringing.

Feeling of Touch or Other Contact

Ghosts can pull covers off you when you are in bed. You may feel the sensation of them sitting on the foot or edge of your bed. They can drape their arms around your waist or shoulders. They can play with your ears or pull your hair. Some ghosts will touch or create a breeze on the back of your neck. I have met female ghosts who like to gently scratch men's backs with their fingernails. This kind of contact usually happens when the ghost has an unusual amount of energy or around the full or new moon.

Environment

The effect an earthbound spirit can have on your environment will vary depending on how much energy that ghost possesses. Following are some of the most common disruptions that can be attributed to earthbound spirits.

Moving or Hiding Objects

I have seen ghosts who are able to move furniture, but it's more common for them to move or hide small items such as keys, checkbooks, paperwork, or jewelry. This is a very effective way for an earthbound spirit to get a reaction from a living person. Think about how stressed you become when you're late for an appointment and your car keys—which you are positive you left on the kitchen table—are missing. Or your anxiety when you're certain you've put your checkbook and bank card in your purse, but find they're not there when you try to use them in a store. Later you may discover them tucked in a drawer or under a pile of paperwork on your desk.

When ghosts are able to move larger objects, the effects can be quite dramatic. In one memorable example of a ghost determined to get his own way, I was called to a nursing home where the staff had completely sealed off one of the rooms—a spacious suite on one of the more private floors. The room was beautifully decorated with an antique bedroom set, including a four-poster bed, a bureau, a dressing table, and nightstands. The nurse who was taking me around explained that the furniture had belonged to a very wealthy former patient who had actually commandeered several rooms as a private "suite" while he was a resident in the home. Before his death he had given his children very specific instructions as to which items of furniture each was to have. When their dad died, the kids, not wanting the outdated pieces, donated them to the nursing home. That was when the trouble started: No matter where the staff moved a piece of furniture, the next morning it was right back in the room where it had started. They had tried moving just one piece of the set at a time; they had tried moving each piece into a different room simultaneously. No matter what they did, by morning the furniture was all back in the room where it had started.

I found the ghost of the older man hanging around in the common room on the main floor. He was enraged at his children and, by this point, at the staff for continuing to try to "give away" his bedroom set. Despite my best efforts, I could not convince him to cross over. The staff have since found that simply keeping the pieces of the bedroom set together in one room seems to pacify him. I imagine that if they ever really need that room, I'll be hearing from them again. I hope this time the ghost will be ready to leave.

Temperature Changes

Fleeting temperature changes in certain rooms may be a sign of an earthbound spirit's arrival or departure. Now, people do tell me that they're sure they have a ghost because a particular room is "just cold/hot *all the time*." In these cases, it's more likely that the room has a northern exposure and lack of sunlight, or is simply drafty or overly sunny. But feeling a sudden draft move through the middle of a room, or sensing a warm spot where there isn't a pool of sunshine, may indicate that you are not the only being in the room.

Electrical or Mechanical Malfunctions

These problems show up equally in homes and businesses. The energy from an earthbound spirit can be disruptive to any electrical device, including televisions, computers, heating or air-conditioning systems, and elevators. In your home, you may find that your stove turns on and off, lights flicker, lightbulbs burn out or explode, your television has lots of static, your computer crashes, and small appliances break or don't work correctly. You may have troubles with your furnace and hot-water tank, or with air-conditioning units or ceiling fans. Toilets may flush themselves, and doors may swing open or slam shut.

The same types of problems are common in the workplace. I have done work at a number of theaters in the Cleveland area and have discovered that the ghosts in a theater delight in causing the elevator that moves from the stage level down to the basement dressing rooms to stall or get stuck between floors. There is nothing more nerve-racking than having the costume for a quick backstage change stuck on an elevator whose doors refuse to open. On the set of *Ghost Whisperer*, we experience numerous disruptions, from missing scripts to popping set lights to unexplained malfunctions of complicated cameras and equipment.

I remember once when Ted and I stopped at a diner-style restaurant on the way home from an afternoon of attending viewings at several funeral homes close to our home. Ted was intently studying the menu when I noticed the ghost. He was a huge guy, maybe in his forties, wearing the white T-shirt and work pants that you might see on a line cook or counter help. His arms were covered with tattoos, and he had a crew cut and a mean glint in his eye. I saw him stare at one of the waitresses, and then he went to work: Slipping behind the counter, he turned off the coffeemaker, then slid open the door of the cooler before heading through the swinging doors back to the kitchen.

The waitress he'd been staring at stopped at our booth to take our order. She was about halfway back to get our cups of coffee when an older woman, dressed in the same skirt-and-blouse uniform as our waitress, came charging out from behind the counter. "You turned the damned coffeepots off again," she barked. "How many times do I have to tell you to leave the machine on after you make coffee?" Our waitress tried to protest, but the other woman just cut her off and stomped back to the coffeepots, mumbling about how she was going to have to make fresh coffee.

Our waitress was clearly flustered when she went back to the kitchen to place our order. I quickly filled Ted in on what was going on. Maybe ten minutes later, I looked toward the swinging doors of the kitchen just in time to see our waitress coming through them carrying the tray with our food. Right behind her was the guy, and I watched as he tipped the back end of her tray up until our dishes and dinner crashed to the floor.

The poor girl burst into tears, and the sour older waitress came over to us to apologize. She waited on us for the rest of our meal. I didn't have a chance to ask the first waitress if she had perhaps once known a big guy with a crew cut who might have been holding a grudge against her.

I have seen ghosts with enough energy to change information in computers. They might rebook appointments or substitute or delete patient information, especially in dentists' offices. Ghosts are also able to cause malfunctions in X-ray and other medical machines.

Children

Children are extremely sensitive to the presence of earthbound spirits. Imaginary playmates, guardian angels, or "scary people" may sound like figments of young imaginations, but most times they are very real. There are a few typical behaviors you may notice from children living in a house with a ghost.

Physical Ailments

Children under the age of ten may suffer from frequent colds or respiratory infections. Sore throats, ear infections, and asthma may all be common.

Broken Toys

"But I didn't do it!" is the most common cry of a child who lives in a house with a ghost. Child ghosts, in particular, will break toys or turn on battery-operated games. They hide pieces of board games, drain batteries, and stash away beloved stuffed animals.

"Imaginary" Friends

If your child insists that the other little girl who comes every day for tea parties is real, you may want to consider whether or not you are experiencing any other signs of earthbound spirits in your home. A lot of people will discount a child's claims, noting that almost all children outgrow these imaginary playmates. What I point out to such skeptics is that the earthbound spirits most attracted to children are children themselves. And because earthbound spirits do not age chronologically, they are soon left behind as their living playmates grow and develop new interests. Child ghosts will usually move on to another household once the child they are attached to grows older and develops other interests.

Sudden or Unexplained Fears

When children suddenly begin avoiding a particular room or area of the house, or are inexplicably unable to spend the night in their own beds, it's usually a good indicator that something— or more likely, someone—is disturbing their sense of security in their own home.

Pets

If your pet begins exhibiting strange behaviors, it could be an earthbound spirit is bothering it in some way. I have seen mean ghosts kick or pinch animals. They will pull a dog's or cat's tail or try to catch it with a closing door. They will close pets in a closet, or lure them into a forbidden room. If you pay close attention to your pet, you may notice it reacting to empty space as if there were someone there. A dog may bark while staring straight at a bare spot on the wall. A cat may arch its back and hiss in the middle of the room. By carefully observing where your animal is focusing its attention, and how its behavior changes if you remove it from a particular area, you may be able to determine if your pet is reacting to the presence of an earthbound spirit.

Documenting Earthbound Spirits on Film

Many people claim they can capture images of spirits on film. I have received literally thousands of pictures, and I'll tell you that I view most of them with some degree of skepticism. Photographic equipment has become so sophisticated that it's now quite simple for anyone to manipulate a picture.

Once in a while, when I visited homes to clear earthbound spirits, I used to bring my own camera with me. But eventually I realized how uncomfortable that might make clients feel. There I was, a virtual stranger, sitting in their dining room, snapping pictures of the empty wall near the grandfather clock. And so I stopped bringing a camera along.

When people tell me they want to take a picture of the ghost in their house, I advise them to use a simple disposable camera with the highest-speed film they can find (black and white is best) and no flash. Since the film is never out of the camera until it is developed—and since I don't expect that the clerk at the local superstore where you develop your photos will have any idea why you have taken a whole roll of film of your living room drapes—there's is very little chance the exposures will be tampered with. Point the camera in the direction where you sense the ghost is standing and hope for the best.

I have had some success in capturing ghostly entities on film, but the most exciting example for me was when one of the earthbound spirits on the set of *Ghost Whisperer* showed up on film. Jennifer Love Hewitt had just finished an intense scene when someone on the crew noticed a movement in the shadows behind her. The director stopped the shoot and the cast crowded around the monitor to watch the scene as it was replayed. They were shocked when the figure of a person loomed behind Love in one of the frames. The editor working on the scene was stunned and repeatedly asked cast and crew if they were seeing what he was seeing. Everyone agreed that for a fleeting moment, someone—or something—that hadn't previously been there appeared on the film. Love was so astounded that she kept the film. She now shows it to anyone who wonders if there are any real spirits on the set of the show.

12

HOW TO DEAL WITH GHOSTS

Protecting Yourself from the Influence of
Earthbound Spirits

IF YOU feel that you are in the presence of earthbound spirits, there are things you can do to diminish their impact and protect yourself, your family, and your home or business from their potentially harmful energy. None of the rituals or practices I recommend in this chapter will cause any harm or invite any negative energy. While you may not be able to completely clear your environment of ghosts or their energy, any or all of these steps may offer some relief.

I will admit right now that I don't know exactly why certain things work to diminish the energy of earthbound spirits. For instance, I cannot tell you exactly *why* the quince seeds my family sends to me from their small village in Italy prevent ghosts from entering buildings. But I can tell you from my experience that they absolutely *do* work. Because they work for me, I have faith in their power and so I use them. If you find that something works for you, then I do not doubt that it does. Many types of objects—when protected and energized with white Light, intent, and/or prayer—can offer protection.

Some Cautions

Before I jump into the *how-tos* of driving away earthbound spirits, I want to briefly talk about the *do-nots*. Please read this section carefully before you attempt any methods of clearing or protecting your house. Believe me, you don't want to energize earthbound spirits instead of weakening them.

Know Who You Are Dealing With

Any time you invite someone into your home to do metaphysical work, or you obtain items to use for cleansing or protection, I cannot stress enough how important it is to work with someone who has been recommended to you. Don't be shy about getting references; ask if there are local clients you can talk with to find out if they were happy with what was done for them. If practitioners are unwilling to supply references, or if clients had any reservations about how things turned out, try to find another option. Remember, anyone can pay their money and take out an ad in the Yellow Pages. If you are not knowledgeable in this area, you must take care that you do not cause trouble rather than diminish it.

Don't Touch the Holy Water

Since I'm on the topic of cautions here, I want to offer a *huge* one. Do not, under any circumstances, think that you can dispel a ghost by throwing holy water around. If you are a layperson, you should not be determining how to use something meant for a blessing in another kind of service. This sort of disrespectful behavior really ticks spirits off. If you have an ordained minister or a priest visit you to offer a blessing, that's one thing. If you as a layperson just start sprinkling the holy water around, you are simply asking for trouble. I have seen spirits become so enraged that they will use their energy to break things, move things, and otherwise display as much of a physical presence as possible. These are the kinds of situations that are often referred to as "hauntings."

Do Not Talk to, or Yell at, Earthbound Spirits

No matter how tempting it may be to start shouting at ghosts who hide your checkbook or turn the stove on while you're out of the house or break that expensive piece on the furnace (again!), do not raise your voice or acknowledge them. If you do, you are giving them exactly what they want: your attention and your energy. Try to stay calm and minimize your reactions. This may be enough to send a ghost off in search of bigger and better energy sources.

A few years ago, I spoke by phone to a woman and confirmed that she did have an earthbound spirit in her house. The male ghost wasn't causing any big trouble—in fact, he was a pretty laid-back kind of guy. I arranged to visit her home later in the following week. Well, let me tell you, when I arrived five or six days later, if the ghost hadn't had on the same clothes, I wouldn't have recognized him. Instead of a mellow, average Joe, the ghost I encountered was full of attitude, strutting around the house and showing off some remarkable displays of energy. I remember thinking that we weren't even close to a full moon, and I wondered where the ghost had gotten all his energy. I mentioned this to the woman, and she sheepishly admitted that she and a few girlfriends had bought a couple of bottles of wine and had a séance after I had confirmed that there was, indeed, an earthbound spirit in her house.

"We thought we could get him to talk to us," she said. Instead, after several attempts at calling him into the room, the lights started flickering, a small table in the hall tipped over, and two of the wineglasses flew off the table and shattered.

"It scared the heck out of us," she continued. "So we all started screaming at him, 'Just you wait until Mary Ann gets here! You'll be sorry.'"

I simply stared at her. I couldn't believe what she had done. Instead of a meek ghost who would have gone calmly into the Light, I now had to deal with a puffed-up spirit on a power trip.

It definitely took some work on my part, but the ghost finally agreed to leave. Not before telling me, however, that the night of the séance was the most fun he'd had since he was earthbound.

Protecting Yourself from Earthbound Spirits

There are several simple things you can do to help protect yourself from the effects of earthbound spirits and negative energies. If earthbound spirits have just followed you home and have been in your house for only a short while, these techniques may be all you need to get them to leave for good. If the ghosts were in the house before you were or have been there for some time, the following items and rituals may not drive them away for good, but they may weaken spirits' energy and provide temporary relief from the negative energy they can create. There is no harm in following any of these recommendations; in fact, they may be all you need to improve your health, mental energy, and environment.

White Light

Everyone can and should learn how to create the white Light of protection. People who practice metaphysical arts, who work with energy-based healing such as Reiki, or even those who meditate or do yoga are usually familiar with using white Light in their practices to help them feel protected, promote healing, and bring focus.

Even for me, the white Light is not simply a way to release earthbound spirits. I visualize a protective white Light around myself and around my family whenever we travel. I use white Light for extra protection when I enter a hospital or undergo medical procedures. The universe provides this positive energy, and everyone should learn to access and use it. Being able to visualize and send white Light to someone is similar to sending a prayer or a good thought in their direction.

Accessing white Light is as simple as visualizing it. When I first noticed the white Light around an earthbound spirit, it reminded me of the intensely bright lights atop my parents' old home movie camera. I suppose the analogy would be to the flash on any of today's cameras. My grandmother used the setting sun to teach me how to make the Light. The point is that the Light is incredibly bright, but you are able to look into it.

If you have trouble visualizing such a pure, bright light, try this simple exercise: Light a candle and stare at the flame. Focus on the hottest part of the flame, closest to the base of the wick. Now shift your gaze from the flame to a blank wall and imagine you can see the flame as a spot on that wall. Look back at the candle and concentrate again on the flame; then turn to the wall and imagine the same spot of brightness. Repeat this exercise until you can see a bright white spot on the wall. When you are comfortable visualizing this small spot of Light, begin to visualize it growing bigger. There is no need to try to increase the brightness as you make the Light larger.

Once you are comfortable creating this white Light, you can then imagine it surrounding you or anyone you want to protect. You can mentally send it to people who are far away by thinking of them as you concentrate on the Light. If you do healing work—whether conventional or alternative—you should always protect yourself with this white Light to avoid attracting any negative energy from your patients.

Sea Salt

One of the most effective ways to remove negative energy and weaken the attachment of an earthbound spirit to an object is to cleanse the object with sea salt. If you are an avid tag-sale or yard-sale shopper or love to buy or collect antiques, be sure to carry a container of sea salt when you go shopping. Before putting an item in your car, sprinkle it with sea salt. There's no need to make it look like a beach. A little goes a long way!

People who work in places where they have a high likelihood of bringing ghosts home with them should add a handful of sea salt to the final rinse when they wash their clothes. Or you may prefer to fill a misting bottle with water and a couple of table-spoons of sea salt. Before walking out the door, mist the air in front of you and walk through the spray.

Sea salt can be used to protect your property or the outside of your home. Sprinkle some around the perimeter of your yard or put it around the foundation of the house. Some people use sea salt in their office or workplaces. Use *a little* sea salt around your desk or cubicle about once a week. You may also want to take a little sea salt with you when you travel. A thin line of sea salt in a hotel doorway can offer extra protection. Using sea salt like this might not be enough to stop a determined ghost from getting onto your property or into your space, but an earthbound spirit will think twice about crossing such a boundary.

People who do metaphysical work need to be particularly care-ful not to pass along negative energy from one client to another. Card readers, for example, should always have two or more decks of cards so they can regularly clean their decks. If someone has been negative or had a negative reading, a second person can pick up this energy by touching the cards. The same type of cleansing is important for anyone who does healing work, such as massage with stones or energy work with crystals. To clean your items, simply put those that have been used to touch clients in Ziploc bags filled with sea salt. For the most potent cleansing, leave the bags out overnight around the time of a full moon. Do not worry if you're unable to leave the objects in the moonlight; the sea salt alone will do the job.

I had one client who kept putting her crystals outdoors in a bath of sea salt water. When she went out to bring them in the next morning, they'd be gone. The mystery was finally solved when she got up extra early and noticed a huge magpie taking off with her crystal. After that, she put her crystals in their sea salt water bath on an indoor windowsill in the path of some moon-light. It worked just as well.

There are different theories as to why sea salt is such an ef-fective block against negative energy. One is that as a crystalline substance, it is able to receive etheric, or spirit, energy and hold off certain vibrations. Another theory points to the fact that it is not processed, the way table salt is. Others suggest that the connection between the sea and the lost city of Atlantis—whose citizens were protectors and warriors—may explain sea salt's powers.

Once you have used sea salt to absorb negative energies and create a barrier against earthbound spirits, be sure to dispose of it carefully. Do not throw it out in your yard or pour it down your drain. Take it off your property and leave it in a deserted area or pour it down a sewer or storm drain.

Quince Seeds

As I've said before, I'm not sure why quince seeds work for me, but they certainly do. The quince is a fruit related to the apple and pear. It has been cultivated since early Roman times and is grown by my family in the little village in Italy where my grandmother grew up. When my grandmother took me to clear houses, she'd put one of these little brown seeds over every doorway in the house once I told her that the ghost had gone into the Light. Her relatives in Italy sent her a fresh supply every so often, and now they send the seeds to me. Of course simply buying some quinces at your local supermarket, taking out the seeds, and slapping them up around your house will not do a thing. Like any talisman or charm, the quince seeds need to be energized to offer this specific protection. I still don't know how my relatives energize the seeds to discourage ghosts from entering houses, but I continue to have faith in their power to keep earthbound spirits at a distance.

If you are not sure whether or not your home is free of ghosts, you can keep a quince seed or other energized item on your person to hold earthbound spirits at a distance. When I work with people in professions that tend to attract earthbound spirits— nurses, doctors, police officers, bartenders—I give them energized quince seeds, instructing them to carry the seeds whenever they go to work or to a spot likely to host earthbound spirits. Having a quince seed or other energized item with you will prevent a ghost from attaching to you and following you home.

It is *very* important that you do not put these quince seeds up in your home unless you are 100 percent sure that your house is free of earthbound spirits. If you put the seeds over doorways while ghosts are in the house, those ghosts will become trapped. And believe me, you don't want an unhappy earthbound spirit stuck in your home.

Smudge Stick

Another simple technique for removing negative energy and reducing the effects of earthbound spirits in your home or business environment is to cleanse the atmosphere with a smudge stick. These are bundles of herbs, such as sage or sweetgrass, that generate a lot of smoke when burned and have a very distinctive odor. Light the smudge stick using a candle or match and gently blow out the flame so the stick is still smoking. Keep a tray or bowl under the smudge stick so ash and cinders do not fall to the floor as you use it. Walk around your house, from the highest floor to the lowest, waving the smudge stick around the perimeter of all the rooms. Make sure that you have allowed for enough time to smudge the *entire* house in one session. Keep all windows closed and leave them closed for at least one hour after you've finished the house.

Start in the attic, if you can, and end in your basement. If you have an attached garage, don't forget to smudge there. Be sure to smudge behind doors, in corners, in closets, and in cabinets. If the smudge stick goes out—and it will if there's a lot of negative energy in the house—relight it and continue smudging from the spot where it first went out.

You can also fan the smoke so that it surrounds your body. Make sure that it touches all parts of you. When you are finished, place the smudge stick in a fireproof container filled with sand.

Always be sure that the smudge stick is fully extinguished before leaving the room where it is stored.

To get a sense of how effective smudging is for you, be sure to mark your smudging date on a calendar. At first, it may be only five or six days before you realize that negative energy seems to be returning or that the ghost in your house is becoming active again. As soon as you notice either of these things, smudge immediately. Again mark your calendar. Pay close attention to how long it takes before the activity begins again. The more regular you are with smudging, the longer you will be able to go between treatments. Depending on how much of a foothold ghosts have, or how negative their energy is, you may end up having to smudge only once a month or less.

If you smudge on a regular basis and there are ghosts in your home—even ghosts who've been there for a while—you can make them leave. They'll eventually get sick of feeling lethargic and will leave to seek a place where they can get more energy. It's really a question of being persistent and waiting them out.

If you have small children or anyone with breathing problems, such as asthma, make sure they are out of the house while you smudge. Wait until the smoke has fully cleared before you bring them back home.

Blessings

It is never a bad idea to ask an ordained minister, priest, shaman, or other experienced religious leader to visit your home and bless it. The positive energy from such a blessing can help counteract the effects of an earthbound spirit in the home.

Other Forms of Protection

The items and rituals I've listed above are those that have always worked for me personally. I haven't had to try others—and as long as the ones I use keep working, I don't see the need to. Nevertheless, different people use all kinds of things to diminish negative energy. If it works for you, you should do it. Think of ridding your house of this harmful energy as a process of trial and error. Here are some other suggestions that you might like to try:

- **Marigolds.** Stringing a garland of marigolds across a doorway is said to help keep earthbound spirits away from a home. Pick the marigolds at noon, dry, then string them over the tops of doorways. They can also be dried and burned as incense.
- **Cyprus.** Known as the tree of death, cyprus wood is used for protection.
- **Geraniums.** Dry the flowers and make sachets to put in corners and basements.
- **Myrrh.** The oil of this tree has been used for centuries to offer protection. You can find myrrh in oil or incense forms. If you feel that there is negative energy in your home, smudge the rooms with a stick of incense made from myrrh.
- **Rosemary.** Used for cleansing, often in combination with sea salt.
- **Rowan wood.** Also known as mountain ash. I have used this protective wood in children's rooms. You can break small twigs off a tree (be careful, because the berries are very poisonous) and form them into a small cross. Bind the cross together with red yarn or thread. This age-old protective amulet can be carried with you; it's also particularly effective when hung in the doorway of a child's room.
- **Tobacco.** Shredded tobacco leaves (not the processed kind of tobacco found in cigarettes) can be scattered around the corners of your property to offer protection. Be careful that children and pets do not ingest it.
- **Violets.** These beautiful purple-and-white flowers are very good for cleansing and protecting. You can iron a flower between sheets of waxed paper and carry it in your purse or wallet for protection.

13

CURSES AND OTHER NEGATIVE ENERGY

What You Can Do to Prevent, Remove, or Weaken Negative Energy

WHEN YOU hear that a person "has a curse on them," or that a particular location or item is cursed, it can sound very hopeless and maybe a little dangerous. But the most important thing to understand about curses is that they are simply a form of energy. To put it in the simplest way: Energy that is good, or brings a positive force, is called a charm or blessing. Energy that is negative and brings an adverse force is called a curse.

How Someone, or Something, Becomes Cursed

It's important to remember that a curse can be put on only by a living person. People who call me often want to know if an earthbound spirit has put a curse on them, their family, or their home. I assure them that there is no way a ghost can put a curse on anyone or anything.

Every culture and every ethnic group has its own version of a curse. It can be known as a jinx or hex or evil eye. To keep things as simple as possible, I will talk about two general categories of curses: those that I call Old World curses—negative energy specifically put onto someone by a skilled person using certain rituals—and curses that are really more a general accumulation of negative energy.

Old World Curses

There are definitely people who can put on curses, often very particular types of curses. If you go to any major city with ethnic neighborhoods, you will find a number of people with this kind of knowledge. When my grandmother first taught me, at age six-teen, how to remove a curse, I thought that only Italians knew how to release negative energy. And I thought that only Italians could put it on. And why not? All the men and women who came to see my grandmother so she could remove the *malocchio*, evil eye, were from the Old Country.

When I was older and I shook hands with people, I could tell if they had a curse or negative energy on them. My hand would feel uncomfortably tingly—as if it had fallen asleep and was get-ting that pins-and-needles sensation that meant it was waking back up. What surprised me was that I sometimes got this sensa-tion even if the people I was greeting weren't Italian. I was quite curious about this, and luckily I had a lot of friends from different ethnic backgrounds. I asked them all to introduce me to their grandmothers or aunts or great-aunts, most of whom were first-generation immigrants, and I asked these women about the type of curses in their homelands. I learned a lot about curses, as well as how to avoid the unpleasant physical sensation I experienced when I came in contact with cursed people. It also became clear to me that it makes no difference where you come from: A curse is simply negative energy, and it doesn't need to be removed in any specific way. I have successfully taken curses off folks from Germany, Serbia, Russia, and India, among other places. And, although the strength of each curse varied, I removed every one the same way every time.

Old World curses can be very long lasting. It's common for the person who is putting on the curse to put it on an object, usually one made of metal or stone. The person who is sending the curse focuses on the object, rather than the individual, and is able to send a regular flow of negative energy into the cursed person's environment, even from a great distance. Necklaces, particularly those with crosses, are commonly used. I once removed a powerful curse from a woman whose sister-in-law in Italy had sent her a metal picture frame that the woman kept in her living room. It was responsible for negative energy that, over time, made her severely ill.

Negative Energy Curses

A common way for a curse to develop over time is by an accumulation of negative energy. Imagine that I told you I needed minor surgery on a particular date at a particular time, and I asked you to say a prayer for me. If, on that day and time, you paused and thought, *I hope Mary Ann does well*, or even visualized the white Light and sent it to me, then you have sent me positive energy. If instead on that day and time, you paused in your routine and thought, *That Mary Ann is a jerk. She's just no good;* you've just sent negative energy. You have cursed me. It's really that simple. If you can send positive energy to someone, you can also send negative energy.

The truth is, it's going to take a lot more than a single bad thought to make me have a bad day. However, if these kinds of negative thoughts or feelings are directed at someone over and over again, especially with the force of hatred or envy behind them, then there is no doubt in my mind that they will begin to affect that person. Picture the effects of a curse as if you were outlining a picture in a coloring book. You'd take your black crayon and go over the lines of the drawing. The more you went over them, the darker and thicker they'd become. Once you become outlined with negative energy, it becomes easier to attract more negative energy. Every time people have had dark thoughts about you or wished you ill under their breath, the negative energy around you becomes stronger, denser, and more powerful. People who have this kind of negative energy around them frequently say things like "If I didn't have bad luck, I wouldn't have any luck at all," or "I have a black cloud over my head," or "I'm a born loser." Fortunately, this kind of negative energy is usually easily removed.

Some people believe that in order to be able to remove a curse, you need to know how to put one on. My grandmother certainly believed this, and although I was sixteen when she taught me how to take a curse *off*, it wasn't until about four years before she died, when I was nearly fifty, that I finally agreed to let her show me how to put a curse *on*. Honestly, I really didn't want to learn how to put the *malocchio* on someone, and I have never done so. I never will. I don't believe in putting negative energy on someone. I have the utmost respect for the universal law: *What goes around, comes around.* Anyone who intentionally puts out negative energy is guaranteed to receive it back in one form or another.

What a Curse Can Do to You

No matter what kind of curse is involved, it will always affect at least one of three areas: money, health, and relationships. Now, of course, life isn't perfect, and these are all parts of life where it's common to have problems. But if there is a curse on you, your problems will be bigger, they will last longer, and they will cause you more pain. Following are some common types of curses and their most frequent effects.

Curses on Families

A generational curse is usually associated with health in some way. Perhaps the best-known such curse is the one said to be on the Kennedy family. Now, I've never met a Kennedy, so I can't tell you for sure if they are cursed, but it just takes one look at the history of that family, particularly the men, to suspect that they are. I have seen curses that cause the firstborn daughters in a family to be barren. I once took a curse off a man who was in his early thirties. His family curse held that the males in every generation died before turning forty. The man's great-grandfather had died at thirty-eight, his grandfather at thirty-six, two of his uncles in their twenties, and his father at thirty-nine. He didn't want to take any chances. I removed the generational curse and I'm happy to say that he lived for many years after he turned forty. The interesting thing about generational curses is that they do not take effect until the cursed individual turns eighteen.

Personal Curses

Personal curses can cause bad health. If you take medications on a regular basis, such as those for high blood pressure or heart conditions, a curse can affect how these medications are working and cause adverse effects to your health. The negative energy of a curse can also distort X-rays, MRIs, or other photographic scans of the body. Certain curses, particularly those from the Mediterranean countries, often cause problems such as headaches, dizziness, and vision disturbances.

Curses can cause problems in romance. Haven't you ever wondered why so-and-so, who's so terrific, never found the right person to marry? Or why someone has been divorced—from perfectly lovely spouses—multiple times? Curses can send a person spiraling into financial ruin and destroy businesses. Athletes seem to be particularly vulnerable. I have worked with many professional athletes, from baseball players to pro bowlers, to remove negative energy that was having an impact on their careers.

Curses on Objects

Having a cursed object in your possession will have negative effects on you whether the object has been intentionally cursed or simply attracted negative energy by being in the possession of someone who was extremely unhappy, depressed, or sorrowful.

After all, rage and envy are not the only negative emotions. If possessing or touching a certain object makes you feel uncomfortable, trust your instincts! People have all sorts of different reactions to negative energy. Some get headaches; others feel queasy or have stomachaches. I have had people tell me that their palms get itchy or sweaty or hot or cold when they touch an object that has negative energy on it. One of the most famous cursed objects is said to be the Hope Diamond. Many of the owners of this legendary stone died suddenly, committed suicide, or endured great tragedy.

Curses on Places or Organizations

Some of the most commonly cursed places are hotels or bed-and-breakfasts and resorts. I think this is because the hospitality industry is so competitive and has such a potential for unhappy customers. If you are staying in a hotel or other place that seems to have negative energy, take the steps outlined in the previous chapter to help protect yourself during your visit. The same is true when house hunting. I do a lot of work for real estate agents. Houses with curses and earthbound spirits can sit on the market forever. If you do find the perfect house, but are worried because you feel that there is negative energy on the property, remember that the house can be fixed. A curse can always be taken off, and a ghost can always be sent away.

Sports teams and their players are other prime targets for curses. Just think of all the energy in the stands when a hometown crowd roots for their team and sends negative energy toward the rival visitors. Sports curses are legendary. There was the Curse of the Bambino in Boston, there is the Billy Goat curse in Chicago, and I've no doubt that my hometown teams of the Cleveland Browns and the Cleveland Indians are also cursed.

But it is possible to remove a curse from an organization. I once received a late-night phone call from someone claiming to be calling from the offices of a major sports team. He'd heard that I could remove curses, and he wanted me to tell him if his team was cursed.

I asked him to call me from wherever the team's franchise paperwork was kept; if I could get a sense of a tangible symbol of the organization—something that could serve as a focal point for negative energy—I could give him an answer. Several hours later, he called back. I told him that there was a curse on the organization —not on the players or the field or the stadium. He asked me if this meant that if I took the curse off, the team would start to win. I replied that I couldn't guarantee any of that—it depended on how good a team he had. But if I removed the curse, at least they wouldn't have to overcome negative energy to win.

He was silent for a few minutes, then asked if I could fly out to the team's home offices the next day. Now, October is the absolute busiest time of the year for me. I usually have more than forty speaking engagements lined up months ahead of time. So I said no. After another long silence, he asked me if he would have to fly the whole team out to me to have the curse taken off.

I explained again that the *team* wasn't cursed, the *organization* was. I told him that if he could get me the paperwork that defined the team as an organization, I could take the curse off. And that is how, a few days later, I came to find myself sitting aboard a corporate jet at a gate in the Cleveland airport. I set up all the items I needed to remove a curse, and the manager took an impressive leather-bound document from a large manila envelope and handed it to me.

I was actually worried about having to put the oil on the leather cover, so I asked him to put the document back in the envelope— after all, there was no need for me to examine the paperwork. He did, and in about three minutes I removed the curse from the organization. I went back home, the plane flew back east, and I can tell you that the team proceeded to delight generations of rabid fans by defeating their historic archrivals in an unprecedented winning streak the likes of which had not been seen literally in decades.

Whenever people ask me if I've done work for a particular team or athlete, I tell them what I truly believe: Removing negative energy is always helpful, but to win at anything, you still need to be the team that played the best that day.

How to Remove a Curse or Negative Energy

Anyone can attempt to remove a curse or negative energy from another person. Nothing I recommend in this section can cause anyone any harm. Whether or not you can feel the presence of the negative energy, whether or not you're sure you're doing the ceremony the right way, doesn't matter. You cannot mess up. If you don't do the ceremony the right way and the energy doesn't come off, you haven't made it worse. If you do the ceremony on people who have no curse, you won't put one on them. There really is no reason not to attempt this.

When I lead workshops teaching people how to remove curses and negative energy, they often tell me that, although they have followed all the steps, nothing happened. As you gain experience and become more comfortable with energy work, it will become easier to tell if you have removed the negative energy. If you are in doubt when you first try these techniques, it's still safe to assume that you have been successful. When I've been able to follow up on workshop participants' attempts to remove negative energy, I can report that at least 90 percent of the time they succeeded.

Items You Need for Negative Energy Removal

- **Candle.** I prefer white, but any color can be used. The flame quickly takes up and releases energy. It burns up negative vibrations in the area. It can also serve as a focus for your mental energy. Preparing your candle with your own energy will help you use it to remove negative energy. Rub holy water or oil on the surface. Start in the middle and apply to each end, stroking first upward and then downward. As you are doing this, let your energy run from your hands to the candle with thoughts that this candle will light the way for you. Focus on how the bright white Light of the candle will help to disperse the negative energy out to the universe.

- **Glass dish**. This dish must have at least three separate, divided sections.

- **Holy water.** Pure holy water is best; placing a few drops in regular water will make all the water holy, but it won't be as strong. While you should never use holy water intending to drive out an earthbound spirit, it is safe to use on a cursed person, object, or land.

- **Powders.** Choose any of these powders with protective benefits: garlic, sulfur, cosmic dust (available at metaphysical shops), or ashes from palm, birch, mountain ash, or pussy willow. To get ash from the trees, cleanse (with holy water) a glass pie plate or heat-resistant bowl. Burn the dried leaves or wood. Store the ash in a tightly sealed glass jar. Do not mix the ash of different trees; use a different jar for each type of ash.

- **Herbs.** Any of the following herbs are useful for removing negative energy: *rosemary* or *pennyroyal*, for strength, protection, and peace; *celandine* for protection, escape, and releasing entrapments; *garlic* for healing, exorcism, and protection; *dill* for protection and neutralizing envy; *alfalfa* for protection against money loss; *vervain* for protecting love or money and promoting healing.

- **Oil.** Use virgin olive oil or fragrant oils. You can purchase prepared oils in metaphysical shops. Some you may want to explore using include anise, bergamot, civet, drive away evil, five finger grass, free from evil, and geranium.

- **Incense** helps disintegrate negative energy and purify the atmosphere. Geranium, sweetgrass, sage, and frankincense are commonly used.

- **Protective amulet, talisman, or totem.** These objects can all be energized with stored psychic energy and used as protection against negative energy. I always use a cross or a rosary. If you choose to use one of these, or a saint's medal or something similar, it should be blessed or contain a relic. If you have a new rosary, have it blessed by an ordained priest or minister. If you prefer to use some other symbol of protection, you can consider any of the following:

- An *amulet* is a natural object left in its virgin state such as a stone, gem, shell, or piece of wood. Common forms are pyramid, squares, and spheres. To energize an amulet, direct your thoughts, emotions, words, and breath toward it. Natural life forces such as sun, water, wind, rain, and lightning can also be used. An amulet that is worn on the body is constantly energized by the wearer's emotions.

- A *talisman* is an inanimate object that brings changes in environment and lifestyles. It can be made from a piece of paper or handmade or created by the owner. It is constructed to attain definite results using symbols, astrological signs, hieroglyphs, or special words. To energize a talisman, gaze at it, rub it between your palms, and place it under the sun, stars, or near water. Once it is energized, it should be safely wrapped and carried or worn by the owner until it is ready to be used.

- A *totem* is an object, plant, or animal that serves as a sacred, personal talisman. Totems may appear in dreams or visions to warn individuals of danger, bring them strength, heal their bodies, or bring them abundance. Symbols of your totem can be worn on your body or clothing, or carried.

- **Guard stones.** During negative energy removal, keep one of these stones with you for additional protection: amethyst, black tourmaline, malachite, obsidian, or turquoise.

Remember: It is very important to cleanse each object after each use.

How to Remove Negative Energy from a Person

Although this can be done anywhere, it is easiest if you have a table to place your items on and a chair for the person to sit on.

1. Ask permission of the person to remove the negative energy. The person does not have to believe in what you are doing but must give you permission.
2. Place yourself in the white Light (see page 214).
3. Light your candle and place it on the table.
4. Be sure you are carrying or wearing your talisman, your amulet, or a symbol of your totem.
5. Fill one section of the glass dish with *liquid* (either oil or holy water), one section with *herb,* and the third section with a *powder.* This is the minimum number of items you must use. You may choose to use more, but you must at least have one choice from each of the three categories.
6. Seat the person at a table with arms resting on the surface, wrists facing upward. Stand behind the person with your hands on the shoulders.
7. Ask the person to look into the candle flame or focus on a point in front of him or her. Subjects should think pleasant thoughts or say a prayer—whatever they are comfortable with that will promote positive energy.
8. You should feel the release of negative energy in the palms of your hands as soon as you place your hands on the person's shoulders. Call upon your spirit guide, angels, or archangels to help you remove the negative energy. Using your fingers, place a dab of liquid, herb, and powder on the person's wrists. You can also place a dab of each item on the person's forehead (over the "third eye").
9. Visualize a dark shadow coming off the person, starting at the feet and working toward the top of the head. As the negative energy leaves the body, you release it to the universe and replace it with white Light.

10. Visualize the white Light pushing the energy from the floor upward.
11. When you cannot feel the negative energy anymore, it is removed. If you choose, you can repeat the steps a second time.

It is important that the energy is released into the universe. Do *not* try to send the negative energy back to the person who sent it. You are not the curse police. And trust me, you do not want this kind of energy on your karma!

How to Remove Negative Energy from an Object

1. Place yourself in the white Light (see page 214).
2. Light your candle and place it nearby.
3. Be sure you are carrying or wearing your talisman, your amulet, or a symbol of your totem.
4. Fill one section of the glass dish with *liquid* (either oil or holy water), one section with *herb,* and the third section with a *powder.* This is the minimum number of items you must use. You may choose to use more, but you must have at least one choice from each of the three categories.
5. Place a dab of the liquid, the herb, and the powder on the item. If it's a small object, one dab should be enough. If it's larger, use more. For instance, if you are removing negative energy from a car, place a dab on the front bumper and the back bumper. If you are working with a bedroom set, each piece must be dabbed individually. For a mirror, place a dab of the mixture in each corner or one at the top and bottom and on each side. If the object is made of something that cannot have the mixture touch it, place the item in a plastic bag or wrap it in plastic and continue as before.
6. Place your hands on the item and visualize white Light pushing the negative energy off and moving it upward.

For a mirror, visualize the white Light lifting the negative energy up from the surface in a sheet. Send the negative energy into the universe.

How to Remove Negative Energy from a House or Building

1. Place yourself in the white Light (see page 214).
2. Light your candle and place it nearby.
3. Be sure you are carrying or wearing your talisman, your amulet, or a symbol of your totem.
4. Fill one section of the glass dish with *liquid* (either oil or holy water), one section with *herb*, and the third section with a *powder*. This is the minimum number of items you must use. You may choose to use more, but you must have at least one choice from each of the three categories.
5. Place a dab of liquid, herb, and powder over the entrances to the structure.
6. Determine where the center of the building is. You do not need an exact measure. Eyeball the space and make your best estimate.
7. Visualize the white Light pushing up the negative energies. Picture it starting in the basement and moving up through the building's center.
8. If the building has a lot of floors, you may want to repeat steps 6 and 7 on several of the floors.

How to Remove Negative Energy from a Piece of Land

1. Place yourself in the white Light (see page 214).
2. Light your candle and place it nearby.
3. Be sure you are carrying or wearing your talisman, your amulet, or a symbol of your totem.
4. Fill one section of the glass dish with *liquid* (either oil or holy water), one section with *herb*, and the third section with a *powder*. This is the minimum number of items you must use. You may choose to use more,

but you must have at least one choice from each of the three categories.

5. Dip a cotton ball in each section of the dish. Start with liquid so the other substances will stick to the cotton.

6. Bury one of these cotton balls about an inch below the surface in every corner of the property. If you are unable to bury the cotton balls at the very perimeter because of water, rocks, or dangerous terrain, just place them as close as you can.

7. Move to the middle of the property and bury one of the cotton balls there.

8. Visualize the white Light coming up from the ground and pushing the negative energy upward and into the universe. Visualize the energy rising higher and higher until you cannot see it in your mind's eye anymore.

A Final Word

I HAVE SPENT more than fifty years seeing and talking to ghosts. And from the moment it became clear that this would be my life's work, I've felt that it was my responsibility not only to help earthbound spirits cross over into the Light but to educate the living as well. Each time I give a lecture or offer a workshop in removing negative energy or take calls on a radio show or brainstorm with the writers on *Ghost Whisperer* about a new story idea, I have the opportunity to demystify the world of earthbound spirits and help people understand that there is often no reason to fear ghosts. I have the chance to show them that there are ways to avoid inviting earthbound spirits or negative energy into their lives.

The stories and information in this book were intended to give you insight into the world of earthbound spirits and provide you with the kind of in-depth information you need to deal with them. I hope you've come to the conclusion that, as mysterious as it may at first seem, the world of ghosts is actually quite mundane. If you can begin to appreciate just how ordinary their existence can be, you're on the way to understanding how I can take for granted my constant immersion in their world. And yes, I've certainly found myself in any number of exciting, hilarious, awkward, and even unnerving situations, but at the end of the day—it's just what I do.

After finishing this book, you should know that when you die (and we all will someday), crossing into the white Light is un-questionably the right thing to do. Of course you will have the choice whether or not to go. If, for some reason, you decide to stay, I hope that you'll remember what I've told you about finding the Light on your own: Just head to a funeral home where a service is in progress!

If I've done anything with this book, I hope I've offered you some important instruction for your life *and* afterlife. I'm going to assume that I won't run into any of you as spirits, that you'll all take responsibility for crossing over and moving on to whatever awaits us in the Light.

I'm just one person, and as far as I know there are countless earthbound spirits. The most important reason for writing this book was to tell you what to expect and how to act when confronting ghosts. If I've done a good job, I expect that in time I'll be able to confirm, and you may be able to sense, the benefits. There will be fewer spirits who get stuck here on earth, fewer unwanted ghosts vexing the living, and more positive and less negative energy.

Acknowledgments

Writing this book has been an adventure for me. In the past ten years I wrote and self-published three books that are now out of print. With this book there's been a whole team of people involved and I want to acknowledge everyone that helped me, both in writing this book and in getting to the point where it was possible.

My most sincere thanks to James Van Praagh, for his friendship and for having the vision to know that a television series based on the kind of work I do would be a hit.

To Bella Bajaria and Doug Prochillo for great dinner parties, never getting tired of my stories, and connecting me with the talented John Gray, whose writing and directing skills make *Ghost Whisperer* come alive each week. I'm very grateful to Jennifer Love Hewitt, "my little ghostbuster in training." Thank you for sharing your ghosts with me and for being such a wonderful actress. Special thanks to CBS and the producers of *Ghost Whisperer*, Ian Sanders and Kim Moses, for their creative talents and for making Friday night television so compelling; and to the cast and crew for all their tireless energy and hard work.

To Jennifer Gates, my book agent with Zachary Shuster Harmsworth, who saw the television special on *Ghost Whisperer* and knew my work would be appealing to anyone who questions what lies beyond death. She was persistent in convincing me that a book was needed on this subject. Thank you, Jen. You are so smart and special.

To Melanie Murray, my editor at Grand Central Publishing,

who made me feel so comfortable and asked all the right questions about the hows and whys of earthbound spirits. I appreciate your patient guidance through every step of this process.

To Scott Schwimer, my Los Angeles attorney, who always knows how to calm me down and put my mind at ease. You are so knowledgeable and you have such a great sense of humor. My conversations with you always end in laughter.

To Jill Stern—I could not have done this without you. Your writing skills are amazing. Thank you for keeping me sane while I was driving you insane. You gave all my ghosts life on the pages of this book.

To Louis McClung, of Lusso Cosmetics and Photography, for always making me look so good.

I also want to express my love and gratitude to my husband, Ted, and my daughters, Amber and Tara, for all the love, positive energy, and support. Thanks to all my relatives and friends for your ongoing belief and encouragement. Thank you to all of my clients over the years—both alive and dead—whose stories and photos I share. A big "thanks y'all" to Larry and Phillis Townes for your friendship and hospitality; to Kevin and Eleanore McLaughlin for years and years of warm companionship; to Dominic Cerino and Carmen Cerino of Carrie Cerino's Restaurant for your generosity and your delicious calamari; and to David Powers for all your hard work early on.

To all the folks in TV and radio who never seem to tire of my stories and are happy to give me the chance to communicate with listeners all over the country, including Terry Moir and the *Good Company* cast and crew at WKYC/NBC in Cleveland, Ohio. Also in the Cleveland area, thanks to Phillip "Trapper Jack" Elliot at WDOK; Joe Cronauer, Brian Fowler at the Mix 106.5; Jim Mantel at WGAR; and George Noory of *Coast to Coast*—thank you all for sharing your audience with me. Thanks to Mark Dawidziak at the *Cleveland Plain Dealer*, Rich Heldenfels at the *Akron Beacon Journal*, and Eric and Ginger Burnette.

Finally, and most important, I give thanks to God for giving me this gift and the wisdom to use it well. I am so blessed.

About the Author

MARY ANN WINKOWSKI was born and raised in Cleveland, Ohio, and still lives there with her husband, Ted, and Just Fred, their red-and-white cat. She also has two grown daughters. Born with the ability to see, hear, and talk to earthbound spirits, Mary Ann works as a paranormal investigator, helping people all over the world to resolve their problems and questions regarding ghosts or negative energy. She is also a consultant on the CBS hit television show *Ghost Whisperer*. To find out more about Mary Ann, visit her Web site: www.maryannwinkowski.com.